NEW THOUGHTS ON TAROT

NEW THOUGHTS ON TAROT

TRANSCRIPTS FROM THE FIRST INTERNATIONAL NEWCASTLE TAROT SYMPOSIUM

Edited by Mary K. Greer and Rachel Pollack

Hilary Anderson, Ph.D.   Amber Jayanti

Angeles Arrien   William C. Lammey

Eileen Connolly, Ph.D.   Rachel Pollack

Gail Fairfield   Nicolas Tereshchenko

Mary K. Greer   James Wanless, Ph.D.

NEWCASTLE PUBLISHING CO., INC.

North Hollywood, California

1989

CONTENTS

PUBLISHER'S NOTE

All the essays in this anthology are transcriptions of tape recordings of the talks given at the first Newcastle International Tarot Symposium, held in Los Angeles, September 2–4, 1988. In editing them for publication, care has been taken to retain much of the natural informality of the presenters' talks. In doing this, it is our hope that some of the feeling of spontaneity and good will which pervaded this symposium will come through on the printed page.

INTRODUCTION

The Labor Day weekend in 1988 was hot, over 100 degrees every day, yet inside the Los Angeles Sheraton Plaza La Reina, an unusual group of people had gathered. This was not the ordinary conference of dentists or statisticians, but the First International Newcastle Tarot Symposium. Inside the Sheraton's air-conditioned conference rooms, hallways, dining room, and even the lobby, were the workshops, lectures, discussions, rituals, and live readings of a band of Tarot enthusiasts. Not only were the speakers luminaries in the field (Hilary Anderson, Angeles Arrien, Eileen Connolly, Gail Fairfield, Mary Greer, Amber Jayanti, Bill Lammey, Rachel Pollack, Nicolas Tereshchenko, Jim Wanless, and surprise guest Peter Balin), but the attendees themselves were as dynamic and exciting a group of Tarot teachers, counselors, readers, and artists as you'll ever find. Every minute was a feast! Every person there had something to offer, and did.

There have been other Tarot symposiums. The idea originated with Angeles Arrien, who offered the first symposium in 1979 and continued it as a yearly tradition until 1986. She also sponsored the first issues of the *Tarot Network News* in an effort to link people working in the field. A Tarot symposium is a special event, for most of us work alone, studying and writing about the cards and reading for ourselves or others in private. Except for a class or workshop now and then, we rarely meet people interested enough in the Tarot for a real conversation.

In addition to the lectures presented, which make up this book, there were also more loosely structured workshops at the symposium. In these workshop settings everyone began to contribute to the experience as a whole. For instance, Gail Fairfield gave a workshop on using the Tarot to recover from addictions. She demonstrated the ways in which readings can help people face their addictions and make decisions about overcoming them.

During the symposium, one of the attendees referred to a Tarot deck being prepared in braille. This is only one example of how Tarot is moving into new areas, and it shows the determination to make the Tarot accessible to the widest possible public. It also shows recognition of the Tarot as a medium for serious study and growth.

The warmth and sense of community began on Friday evening, with everyone getting together informally in the main room. After Jim Wanless introduced the speakers, Amber Jayanti lighted candles for the Jewish Sabbath and sang a blessing. On Saturday night Alaina Zachary, Mary Greer, and Rachel Pollack led a ritual based on ancient Egyptian initiation. A living Tarot reading followed, with people volunteering to become the cards in a Celtic Cross reading on the future of Tarot. It was comical, with some of the "cards" making speeches, singing, even dancing their parts, but it also reminded us all of why we had come. And then Eileen Connolly gave an original dramatic presentation, with each of the teachers acting out the Tarot trumps, using short scripts prepared by Eileen. We all knew this was going to happen; what came next was a surprise. One by one, volunteers coached by Eileen rose up from the audience to speak, and sometimes sing, tributes to each of the speakers.

Some of the lectures you will read in this book were written out beforehand; others were given from notes. In their own ways, they convey the very personal quality that marked the weekend. On one hand, we find Eileen Connolly's story of longing for the New Age many years before it began, as well as her introduction to Tarot at the age of twelve by an old Romany woman. And on the other, Jim Wanless makes himself a case study in using the Tarot to get over the fear of relationships.

In a way, the Newcastle Symposium began with a class taught by Mary Greer and Rachel Pollack the previous year, on the other side of the country. Mary was teaching at the Omega Institute in New York State and asked Rachel (who was visiting her father, near Omega) to join her for an afternoon session. The class developed into a discussion of people's experiences with the cards.

Afterwards, Rachel and Mary discussed the idea of doing a book that would consist of taped classes, so that people unable to take workshops would get a sense of the experience. Rachel returned to Europe and Mary to California, and for a while the project remained a vague idea, with Mary suggesting that they might invite a few other teachers to give the sessions more scope. But when she suggested it to Al Saunders, the publisher of Newcastle Books, Al saw the possibility for something larger. And so Riley Smith and Julie King, the symposium organizers, began their massive and heroic task, without which the Newcastle Symposium—and this book—never would have come to life.

The official theme was work-in-progress, a chance for the writers/teachers to talk about their current projects. Because of this emphasis on the new, the symposium became something more than a presentation of individual work. It highlighted the developments in Tarot over the last two decades. In a way, it recapitulated the Tarot's history, for it showed the vitality of three major trends: the exploration of esoteric tradition, the emergence of readings as a tool in psychology and healing, and the emergence of new decks, many with radically altered images. For a long time, people assumed these trends were at odds with one another, especially the first two. Esotericists considered readings impertinent, while some psychologists looked upon the occult as irrelevant to ordinary life. And many people thought of the new decks as not really Tarot. The Newcastle Symposium demonstrated that these artificial barriers have fallen.

New decks were definitely a theme at the symposium. Not only were they the subject of Rachel Pollack's talk, but a number of people brought decks they had created themselves. Two speakers presented their own decks at the symposium. While both were solidly in the occult tradition, neither hesitated to enter new territory, even creating entirely new cards.

Eileen Connolly is the author of many books, including *Tarot: A Handbook for the Apprentice*, one of the major books which launched the Tarot revival. As well as being published on its own, her new deck, previewed in her section here, will appear in her forthcoming book, *Tarot: The Handbook for the Master*. A deck can encapsulate a lifetime of teaching. When Eileen's son Peter was a child and learning to draw, she knew he would one day help her create her own deck. The Connolly Tarot was a long time in coming, and Eileen must have had to use the same remarkable patience she showed in her wait for the outside world to acknowledge the New Age ideas and pioneers she had known since childhood.

The Connolly deck follows the Kabbalist tradition in Tarot, partly drawing on the imagery created by A. E. Waite and P. C. Smith in the famous Rider deck. Strength is card 8, as in the Rider deck and its original inspiration, the deck of the Hermetic Order of the Golden Dawn. The Lovers shows the man, woman, angel, and Tree of Life from the Rider deck and the later B.O.T.A. deck. But Connolly takes this tradition further, making the scenes more dynamic, the people in the cards more psychological, and using fewer abstract symbols. For example, Eileen describes the Charioteer's eyes as "full of pain." While the cards come from a tradition, they do not hesitate to present new images. Two figures appear in the Hermit; the Moon shows an occult master who steps away from his pool of contemplation, while "his subconscious" watches him. The Star also is radically different, with the Tree of Life referring back to the themes developed in the Lovers. Two cards are renamed as well as redesigned. Death becomes Transition, the Devil becomes Materialism. Interestingly, these two cards have traditionally contributed to the sensationalist use of Tarot in films and books, as described by Hilary Anderson. Those of us involved with Tarot have always known that Death does not indicate someone dying, and that the Devil signifies bondage to illusions rather than some actual demon with goat hooves and horns. The Connolly names and images bring out the essential themes and take away the fearsome qualities.

Nicolas Tereshchenko's Cosmos Tarot deck has recently been published in France, along with his book on the Tarot. The published deck follows a modern esoteric trend by including various symbols and written information around the edges of the cards. There are I Ching hexagrams as well as Hebrew letters, Golden Dawn titles and Latin names, geometric forms and elemental symbols. It also includes an almost mirror image of the Fool, with the boy, the dog, and the crocodile facing left instead of right, as in the Fool itself. The only difference comes in the Hebrew letter on the boy's bag, Shin on the first version, Aleph on the second. He refers to this division of the original card as Furca the Fool (0) and The Ape of Thoth (22).

The Cosmos Tarot is bright and exciting, with a wealth of detail and symbolism. And yet, Nicolas has already gone daringly beyond it, to create an entirely new trump, the Drowned Sleeping Titan (23). Or rather, it seemed new to Nicolas when he found himself receiving flashes of this picture. This rising up out of the unconscious must be the only genuine way to bring a new image into something as complex as the esoteric Tarot. And the proof for Nicolas of its validity came—paradoxically—when he discovered that it wasn't new at all, that a description of what he had seen in his mind could be found in the inner workings of the Golden Dawn. The Hermetic Order was a Rosicrucian system of ceremonial magic and initiation. As Nicolas describes in his talk, it contained three grades of development, with a voluminous amount of information for each of the levels in these grades. The Middle Order had three degrees, the second of which was called Adeptus Major. As the middle degree of the Middle Order,

Adeptus Major could be described as the mid-point of the adept's development. And it was when he was reading the initiation for this degree that Nicolas came upon the secret and neglected trump, the Drowned Sleeping Titan, the description of which so closely matched his own intuitive conception.

Despite this validation Nicolas stayed true to his own version of the card, including details from the Enochian Alphabet of Dr. John Dee, described in his talk. This link to a magician from the English Renaissance shows the traditional roots of a development which we might describe as the newest and most radical presentation at the Newcastle Symposium.

Angeles Arrien's work on the Tarot has always shown a mix of tradition and radical departures. Her book, *The Tarot Handbook*, contains her interpretations of the Thoth cards, designed by Aleister Crowley and painted by Lady Frieda Harris. Crowley's teachings form one of the pillars of modern occultism. While respecting Crowley, Angie nevertheless took a daring approach, deciding that the pictures existed independently of their original conceptions. By giving the cards a psychological interpretation, she has brought them into the contemporary Tarot Renaissance, a movement she herself helped to launch.

Angie's talk at the symposium shows another kind of blending of the old and new. Going far back beyond the modern esoteric movement, she looked at the roots of symbols, identifying five basic forms found all over the world. These symbols pervade tribal art, but we also find them on calling cards and corporation logos. Angie's talk demonstrates the connections we can make between the Tarot and different levels of culture.

The primary development in contemporary Tarot has been in readings. We have come a very long way from the simple formulas once found in popular instruction books. The Newcastle Symposium shows how useful a tool readings have become, not only for self-knowledge, but for transformation. For when we know ourselves, and why we do the things we do, we can begin the process of deliberate change, using the Tarot images to help us move into new ways of being.

To do this work we need to trust the images themselves. First of all we need to believe that they contain genuine symbols, that is, representations of reality. Bill Lammey's talk demonstrates the value of such trust. While his work clearly builds on Tarot tradition, it just as clearly seeks to base itself on the essential truths found in the cards and their structure. He describes how he asked himself over and over, "Why twenty-two? Why twenty-two?", not simply accepting the various theories—which usually refer to something outside the cards, such as Kabbalah—but seeking some fundamental structure within the Tarot itself. If we can get inside the cards, Bill says, then we will not need to memorize lists of interpretations. The pictures themselves will teach us their meanings. Bill gives us one of the finest definitions of the psychological Tarot: a rational system for interpreting intuitive information.

Just as Bill Lammey describes the value of trusting the images, Gail Fairfield demonstrates the importance of trusting the specific readings we do with them. In their speeches and workshops, both teachers stressed a fascinating aspect of readings. The particular cards we get depend partly on the meanings we assign to them. If you make a decision that the Hanged Man means peace and security, then it will come up in readings dealing with that subject. But if you decide that the Hanged Man signifies tension, or necessary sacrifice, then it will appear in entirely different contexts. This situation, observed by many Tarot readers, suggests a vast area of Tarot research, so far largely unexplored.

Amber Jayanti demonstrates for us how the Qabalistic Tree of Life can be thought of as a cosmic computer used to store, organize, and manipulate data. The twenty-two Major Arcana are the computer's keys, which give us access to our deepest "programming." Amber says that with these Keys we "unlock the doors of higher consciousness." As in her book, *Living the Tarot*, Amber presents her unique system for working with the cards, not by doing readings, but by using one card at a time and applying its qualities to our lives. She focuses on practical suggestions for integrating the teachings of each of the Major Arcana into daily living.

Both Mary Greer and Rachel Pollack stress the ways in which Tarot stimulates creativity and innovation. Through these images we can synthesize underlying truths among diverse fields of knowledge and thus not only bridge them but evolve new levels of understanding. To Mary, healing emotional pain is crossing such a bridge to create a new reality. Tarot allows us to visualize, plan, and realize the necessary steps in the creative process.

Gail Fairfield's talk gives a sense of the woman herself. She is direct, down to earth, committed to helping people deal with their lives. The talk is entitled, "Creating, Maintaining and Enhancing Relationships," and it gives us clear, sensible techniques as well as demonstrating a recent development in Tarot readings. We no longer seek information alone, for this can leave us with a sense of powerlessness. Instead, we use readings to give us the means to make changes in ourselves and our situation.

Both Mary Greer and James Wanless take this a step further. They show us how we can choose the cards we need instead of waiting to see whether they emerge in a particular reading. Mary's technique of "healing emotional pain" involves going through the deck and choosing those images that embody our fears, desires, and experiences. In a sense, she shows us how to construct our own readings.

Jim Wanless's way of working with the cards involves choosing only two or three Majors but working with them in an intense dialogue. When we know the Tarot well we can designate specific cards as aspects of ourselves. In Jim's own case, he used the Emperor and the Fool to signify his ambivalence to committed relationships. Having set them up as opposing parts of his psyche—his adult and his child—Jim allowed them to speak "independently," arguing with, attacking, and ridiculing each other until at last they found some way of going beyond the split to a new approach. Jim describes how this resolution in his psyche brought about enlightened changes in his life.

Jim Wanless "lectures" in a very lively and personal style, creating an immediate bond between himself and his listeners. His talk gives us a glimpse of the experience of being there, of raising our imaginary cups and drinking a toast—to Tarot, to Mother Earth, to ourselves and one another. The word "symposium," Jim tells us, means "drinking party." The Newcastle party celebrated the Tarot: its generations of students and readers, its explorations and mysteries.

What a change from the times when Tarot seemed to operate as if under a shadow, as Hilary Anderson put it in the last session of the weekend. She suggested freeing ourselves from old projections of the meaning of Tarot by "interiorizing" the once fearful Swords of the deck, so that we can be armed with a new perspective and the determination to defend our "divine Tarot tradition." So it was that those of us who had gathered at the Sheraton represented the new voice of the Tarot. We were the speakers for all those who have chosen these symbolic images as a tool for assisting themselves and others in self-awareness, meeting challenges, discovering purpose and meaning in life's experiences, and creating change in accordance with a vision of wholeness.

Mary K. Greer
Rachel Pollack
January 1989

HILARY ANDERSON

Bringing Swords Out of Depression and Darkness

In RECENT TIMES I HAVE FOUND MYSELF MOVing toward a consideration of where Tarot finds itself among the various esoteric studies, and I find that it is still operating under a kind of shadow. Those who are not developed in the use of the tradition still regard it with a fear of its seemingly awesome, almost demonic power in some readers' hands. Others don't take it seriously at all, while still others scoff at it as being speculative, merely a chance procedure with little merit or credibility. Among the more well known oracular traditions, the I-Ching and astrology have somehow gained more respect with the general public during the last few years. I believe that we must move more confidently toward gaining more appreciation for Tarot tradition from the general public that already has some sympathy for these other esoteric studies.

As I began to work with the idea of Tarot's mixed reputation, the rather chequered career it has endured over the centuries, I wondered what this shadow that seems to cover the cards might be. Why is the Tarot often thought of as "the work of the Devil"? Is it just ignorance, or is there something about the nature of the images, the way they work in our hands, that conjures up a kind of terror that produces the very projection of the Devil card back upon us? And then we must handle this projection as best we can in our individual ways. We are required to handle the

limitation that the Devil image represents, the misrepresentation, the induction into a pandemonium of images pouring from that old instinctual archetype from which we must clear ourselves and the Tarot tradition as carefully and with as much clarity as we can. From the moment the projection of the demonic is upon us, we must do a quick exorcism, or psychologically "become" the image and release it through our own selves—either way, it is a work of deep clearance that requires much self-cultivation and knowledge.

Most of this challenge can be laid at the altar of the Swords suit. For it is with this instrument among the four given to us in the Tarot tradition that the work of clarification can be done. It sits with equality on the table of the Magician, along with Wands, Cups, and Pentacles in most decks. Yet it is with this magical instrument that we readers must bring the bad news, saying that "the struggle is on, slander is afoot in your personal and professional life; conflict is dire; sickness and death are close upon you; stress, strife, quarreling, and all kinds of trouble abound; aggression and violence will befall you; you are under a mood of melancholy; depression, doom, and gloom." At the same time, other suggestions might be made from the same suit, such as to "invoke your intellectual force; meet the challenge with all the might of a fine warrior; initiate change through conquest; triumph without excessive weight of execution; be firm, stand up for your rights; harness your legal stance; be victorious." Each card in the suit carries varied meanings given by various distinguished authors.

For the most part, the tradition as a whole places the Minor Arcana, or minor wisdom court and numbered cards, at variance with the possible origins of the Major Arcana, or trump cards. Even though the aces of the suits sit proudly on the Magician's Table and imply that he has had the use of these particular instruments from the inception of the tradition, whenever that was in the misty past of antiquity, it is nevertheless by common agreement that the suits and the major archetypal images came together as one pack somewhere in the 1400s. Reliable authorities, such as A. E. Waite, Robert O'Neill, William Gray, and many others see these instruments as none other than the Four Hallows of the Grail Legend—the Wand is the Spear, the Cup is the Grail itself, the Sword is of course the Sword, and the Pentacle is the Dish or Circle.[1] If identified with these origins, these talismans probably relate to a much earlier set of symbols of Celtic origin, namely the "Four Magical Treasures" which are the Spear of Lug, the Caldron of Dagda, the Sword of Nuada, and the Stone of Fal.[2] All of this referencing is by way of establishing the authenticity of the suits within a highly respected development of cultural reliance on instruments of great potency from the past, bestowing magical significance and bringing mysterious energies to bear upon any given reading of the cards.

There are some differences of opinion by noted authorities as to whether the Swords suit represents the element of fire or air. Examples of such authorities are Francis King and Stephen Skinner in *Techniques of High Magic*, in which they refer to the dagger-sword as being "a weapon made of iron or steel, forged under heat, sharp and incisive like flame."[3] Others with the same persuasion are Joseph Maxwell in *The Tarot*[4] and Stuart R. Kaplan in *Tarot Cards for Fun and Fortune Telling*.[5] However, for the most part our authors seem to agree that the Swords suit stands comfortably representing the element air, and correspondingly stands for spades in playing cards. If we rely on this last correspondence, we are firmly placing the Swords suit within the work of the intellect, the thinking, rational, and logical working of the mind, along with the opportunity for limiting, placing things at variance, difference, distinction, separation, division, decision-making, and strategical planning.

If seen in the cultural development of Western feudal society, the Swords suit is placed with the Warrior Class, the Nobility; the Cups suit denotes the Clergy; the Coins suit came to stand for the Merchants; and the Wands suit represents the Serfs and Peasantry. This correspondence has been developed by Joseph Campbell in *Tarot Revelations*.[6] Natural implications from this correspondence would include, for example, if one identified with the warrior, one would be required to live by the sword and therefore die by the sword, when under the influence of this suit.

If the last couple of centuries of depth work in Tarot studies has distinguished itself in the interrelation of the various traditions, such as Kabbalistic origins and correspondences, Grail Legend connections, Egyptian origins, and the preservation of gypsy lore in the face of strong hermetic and philosophical foundations kept intact, then this century will, I believe, come to be known as the psychological age, with its gift of correspondence to Tarot's imagery and symbolic heritage. Psychological views on almost all phases of our lives are inherent during our time, and we must not lose the opportunity to look at our tradition in new ways. Perhaps it is not a matter so much any more of whether the pictures are drawn with old symbols or newer versions of the old; whether colors remain the same or are shifted; such arguments as whether Swords belong to fire or air; whether they belong socially to the nobility or the peasantry. Perhaps it is now more important how we relate to and work with Tarot.

Can we develop it deeply within ourselves, so that in our hands the cards become literally our own instruments of knowledge about ourselves and others for whom we read? Can we see these images as representing our selves, internalizing them as functions and parts of our personality? In this respect, the archetypes would not be experienced so much as being "out there," but we would literally see them as twenty-two major energy patterns moving freely within us, and the four suits would become psychomental functions of our consciousness. If we can actually do this internalizing, then the cards can become a true oracle read from "within-out" rather than from "out there." When I say "out there" I mean seeing the cards as related to the externalized world of outer phenomena, which becomes at best a kind of fortune-telling, predictive device always operating at the whim of chance words or thoughts. If we can internalize our imagery system, we can contribute to the discipline with great power and lead the way to deep change and transformation for ourselves as readers, while at the same time providing for an evolutionary shift within the tradition itself.

If we take a rather natural set of correspondences from the psychological work of C. G. Jung, we can see that the four suits sitting with equal value on the table of the Magician, or Hermes, are really Jung's four functions of personality. From this new perspective, Wands become fiery intuition; Cups become watery feeling/emotional content; Swords become airy thinking/rational mind; and Pentacles become sensation modalities.[7] I

think many Taroists already choose to use this correspondence. However, when I continue to see that most reference works still contain connotations of violence and destruction befalling its victims when describing the influence of the Swords suit, then I must begin to look with a psychological perspective at how Swords themselves can be used to clarify. They can turn these meanings into ways through which the victims of the Swords can become victors by using them in a keen intellectual process. This process can provide for such transformation. I believe that the goal of psychology is to analyze or separate the parts so that what is new may emerge with the parts recognized and brought into a new perspective. However, it is important to acknowledge that it is a perspective only, and that a transformation is not always willed into being merely because such a perspective is entertained. To truly make psychological the Tarot archetypes and suits would be an inner task of great magnitude and dimensional elevation in consciousness work.

I believe we can now begin to take the "noble Sword" of the Swords suit and, keeping the old sovereignty classification for strength, self-confidence, and bravery, internalize that great Sword of wisdom in ourselves. We must see, however, that it is a two-edged weapon, part of an interior armor ready to defend as well as destroy. The Sword can convert old antiquated meanings into new terms, clarifying them through the agency of the thinking/rational modality and thereby bringing new translations and interpretations for the tradition's next evolutionary shift.

And what of the old Devil and his work, into which we and our tradition are continually projected? For us to laugh it off is to relieve tension; to be indifferent is unfair, for this diminishes and slights that which is being offered us as an encounter with change. For us to become frightened and hold our tongue, and thereby slip away into the darkness unheard and unseen, is for us to congregate only among ourselves and remain cultish and ingrown. But for us to take up our own magical instrument, our own weapon of intellect, and accept the dignity which is rightfully ours is for us to develop new ways to work with the projection through the essential role of the Swords.

Psychologically, if we are to work with a projection we must look into ourselves and see what part of ourselves is still in bondage to that which is being projected upon us. To see the nature of that bondage, if any, is to see into the nature of the part or parts of our personality held in bondage to an old meaning, a murky, dark aspect of an old archetype which has served the culture well over the centuries. The old Devil has served to keep separations intact, to keep confusion alive, while other negotiations with natural forces and instincts run free. It is an energy pattern that brings instinct to the fore, while at the same time blurring intellect, our thinking/rational function. It literally puts those in bondage to it into a kind of "primary shock," immobilizing or freezing energies which could otherwise be used to take positive action. In the meantime, the trick has been accomplished, and the trickster embodied in the one projecting the image gets away with the trick unchallenged. How good it would be to internalize the great Sword, and when the old projection of the demonic begins to appear, to free up in ourselves any old associations we still harbor, then look the old trickster in the eye, and with the Sword of discrimination and wisdom, with decisive action and strength, move with deft blade to the kill, to the destruction of critical blame, fear, hate, and the disowning of a profound and beautiful tradition. At the same time, with the work of the same Sword, we can triumphantly raise our tradition to its rightful place in our time, fully armed with a new perspective, perhaps more psychological, but also capable of gaining more knowledge about the subtleties of interchanges among the archetypal images and the reader and the readee.

Perhaps such an investigation could throw light upon the shadow cast by the uninitiated on the whole activity of Tarot work, in particular that of divination. Such delving could also bring more information forward with respect to the prophetic gift and the nature of its power when exercised with the aid of a graphically illustrated archetypal image. It is with renewed clarity of thought and vision that we can begin to overturn the harsh sentencing and the critical slashing that usually attends most readings of the Swords, as well as the prognostication of ill fate befalling the victims of their wounding blows, which gives rise to states of depression and melancholy.

After all, I think it is not without great wisdom and foresight that A. E. Waite, in collaboration with the superb artist, Pamela Colman Smith, portrayed the Queen of Swords with butterflies in her crown and cherubs on her throne, suggesting the freedom born of new thought executed by the work of the suit. The image of the butterfly points to a true "metanoia," a renewing of the mind, which in its own natural timing provides for the emergence of new forms.

It has always been of great interest to me to observe how the power of the blade works in other major archetypal trump cards. For example, in the renditions of the Lovers card that still adhere to the older illustration of young Cupid striking his fateful blow, the couple are shown to fall under the power of love, and once bonded in relationship by the agency of his arrow, it was acknowledged in those more classical times that nothing could be done; a kind of fait accompli obtained. It was understood that it was the fate of those so struck to work out the cycle in their personal lives, going through the joys and pain attending relationships in which some levels of choice were not entirely conscious ones. In those early days, we could not ease out of such blows of Cupid's arrow as we can today. Today, his arrow still strikes with great intensity, and it requires much subtlety in relationship skills to remain in a good bonding pattern. It takes equal skill to use the Sword to loosen and adjust the bonds, or in many cases cut the bonds altogether. This frees up the energies for yet another engagement with the power of love.

In another instance, the Justice card illustrates the power of the mighty Sword. So stable is this archetypal image in our consciousness that the basic design of the image has remained almost unchanged through the centuries of Tarot deck production. Traditionally, the Justice figure on the card is usually identified with Athena, the great warrior-goddess who wielded the sharp sword of intellect by which she unfailingly struck a balance between reason and necessity. Psychologically, this archetype still serves to weigh matters coming before her and with a practical turn of mind takes foresighted protective measures so that the demands of necessity are met. It is she who creates and protects inner space and with her

persuasive words honors alien and dark elements, bringing them into reconciliation within the whole.[8]

If we can view the Swords suit psychologically and begin to interiorize it as various thinking/rational functions, the Swords can be utilized as a new power at our disposal to penetrate the shadow over the Tarot tradition and combat the demonic projections cast upon us. From this new perspective, the King of Swords becomes our grand strategist, executing important plans for future development. He sees with the wisdom of a brilliant intellect and therefore is able to negotiate clear and appropriate connections with other disciplines, such as psychology, anthropology, religion, philosophy, the arts, and science, so that Tarot tradition does not become isolated and ingrown. He analyzes and decides on the most appropriate process to gain more respectibility and acclaim for Tarot in our time. During the last few years, I've seen him proudly take the cards down off the musty top shelf of the occult bookstore and bring them out into the open through the work of many writers and artists who have breathed new life into the images.

And what of our Queen of Swords, illustrated in the Waite deck with butterflies in her crown? Is she not an aspect of great Athena herself, a warrior-goddess ready to protect our personal vulnerabilities when we use the cards, ready at the right time to renew our minds so that we can relate to new challenges and take flight when necessary into realms beyond the snare. She has traditionally been described as a widow, a divorced

woman, one who knows the price of personal separation and is able to bear this aspect of life with great understanding. Therefore, it is to her that we can take our personal bondage to old worn-out projections impressed upon us by those who haven't the background to face our King of Swords, with his displays of erudition and eloquence beyond their understanding. It is the Queen who can renew the whole perspective in which we are caught for the moment and can free up any associations with which we might still identify, so that we are cut loose from the projection and can still retain a relationship with the one projectin upon us. She is our inner psychologist, one who can find a personal meeting ground for us, even if it is adjusted to a different aspect.

And what of our Knight of Swords, the one who moves with great energy to perform the necessary tasks, the one who goes to great lengths to see that the borders and boundaries of our newly created space are protected, thereby providing for a safe and secure platform for intellectual debate and interchange. It is he who energetically scouts out new disciplines to compare, new conferences and symposiums to join, and fellows with whom to share new projects and publications. It is he who keeps a watchful eye and the way clear to negotiate new terms of entrance into a new alliance with an old foe, perhaps one who got away with old projections that no longer fit, but now can join in an alliance with mutual respect for gifts and talents hitherto unnoticed. The Knight is ever ready to set forth the terms of agreement with new and old contacts for an expanding interdisciplinary approach to the Tarot.

And what of the young Page of Swords, who is ever vigilant and cognizant of every detail around our personal needs and professional competency requirements? It is he who is meticulous in his work of surveillance, his work of making sure that all is properly prepared, all research is delivered to the appropriate places of negotiation and alliance in thought and structure. He is often seen as a sneak, one who cannot be trusted, and yet without him firmly placed within the new task before us, all things would not be done, and secrets necessary for new undertakings would never be ferreted out. To continue to do the careful work of bringing the tradition into ever new perspective, we will need the Page of Swords working with great speed and accuracy on the computer, the typewriter, and in the art studios to keep pace with other allied growing professional disciplines and transformational arts.

The above four Court figures can be internalized as persons, subpersonalities, or parts of a personality ready to function in the thinking/rational mode of consciousness upon the moment of identification. If we begin to identify with these figures projecting such sharp, precision instruments, we become aware of how concisely issues are laid out and discursively handled. And with a kind of awesome majesty, these persons within us move their great Swords to penetrate the murky, dark, and often fuzzy mind traps of those not so blessed with these inner abilities to bring clarity, analysis, and alternative choices to those under their influence.

The numerical cards of the suit can be seen as mental abilities and acuities in mathematical succession. For instance, to identify with the Ace of Swords is to become one with the ability to think and execute ideas, take decisive action, discriminate between given choices with awareness of their various values and meanings, and to choose correctly, with pragmatic and practical measures emphasized. It often means that one creates a standard and then implements it by precisely cutting or penetrating to the center of the issue, hopefully without excessive weight or heavy-handedness in execution. The Ace is in the symbolic sense the Sword carried or projected by all the Court figures, and is given numerical differentiation and variety in meaning through the succession of the two through the ten.

In identifying with the Two of Swords, two issues or perspectives are held in balance. No decision is necessary. In fact, to let the full tension of opposing ideas or issues develop in one's mind is to provide for the ripening and cultivation of value, an important step in the process. To attempt to hold the tension too long will allow the energy to become stalemated.

The Three of Swords shows decision in action. The balance previously held allows a new direction to be taken, and the way of action

emerges. Since this is altogether new action, there is an emotional component often portrayed in the modern decks with a pierced heart in which thinking and emotional modalities are experienced as somewhat mixed, a combination that always attends new thought.

The Four of Swords is a stabilized stage of mental organization in which the field is at an accumulation point, and a retreat or reorganization can be entertained through inner abilities focused on information gained from other realities, often streaming in from trance or dreamwork. Defense is always prescribed when such information from other dimensions of consciousness is being entertained.

The Five of Swords brings with it an intellectual struggle against failure in the execution of one's plans. Special attention is given to details of strategy where possible or probable defeat is likely to occur, and early negotiations with opposing viewpoints are proposed. Landmark settlements are made so that any misrepresentations are brought to the fore and handled at this time, and any inappropriate sentiment is penetrated so that a new organization of these elements is accomplished.

The Six of Swords brings a mental journey, a strategic transition from former difficulties to a new level of integration and opportunity. An orderly expansion of inner space has been prepared so that vulnerabilities can be confidently and securely defended and that movement toward a future goal can be carefully undertaken.

The Seven of Swords stresses the need for more attention to strategy to provide for larger dimensions of interchange and interdisciplinary study and deliberation. Analysis and technical advancements are accessed, and a knowledge of the field and what will be needed is appropriately surveyed. Anticipated plans for advancement are entertained and precautionary measures are developed.

The Eight of Swords is a search inward to identify individual limitations and restrictions due to past strategies needing re-evaluation. Any difficulties in perceiving the "larger picture" and tendencies toward tunnel vision are checked, and petty details are identified and curtailed so that tendencies toward unnecessary delay and frustration are avoided. An accumulation of factors for success and advancement must be examined inwardly so that orderly development can be achieved.

The Nine of Swords brings with it a natural doubt and distrust of present plans and abilities to proceed, and any tendency to victimization in the way of self-blame, any slashing of the inner critic, is detected. All matters of difficulty are alleviated one by one by the thorough inner probing of the factors pushing for expression that can develop into depression, anxiety, and frustration. Each factor is defeated or turned into useful and practical information within the mind.

The Ten of Swords develops a realization of means by which combined efforts to create a fruitful interchange have led to some disruption of the original strategy proposed and taken forward. All technical and material limits are now analyzed and painfully scrutinized. This marks the end of any illusions about how to proceed, and at last a new perspective for the next collective step is entertained.

For centuries the Swords suit has traditionally represented the opportunity for reader and readee to fall victim to the fate of the cruel Sword more often than sharing in its victories, because the inner technology of creating viable choices and alternatives to matters left to fate were not embraced by most people in earlier times. Today, with the work of psychology and other allied disciplines, we can learn to look at moods of depression and bouts with darkness, gloom, and doom and ask the winning question, "What is the meaning of this?" Then with the Sword that has struck us with the old projection of blame, hate, and separation, that pierced us with deep, dark depression, we can marshal the skill of the warrior to uncover new levels of information with hidden meanings for new interpretations. With a deft and deeper delving, perhaps we will find out what was originally intended, and within those origins, a new unfoldment of information about the power of imagery will be revealed, together with the creation of new ways to work with such energies. Yes, the imagery is powerful, it calls up many patterns difficult to handle and reconcile. There are not only the Devil and the Swords, of course, but there are also other images, such as Death, Tower, and Moon, which can bring us into patterns of response that need much spiritual and psychological clearance. We are living in an age of powerful imagery manipulation in television and theater, as well as in almost every other area of our lives. The profound imagery system of the Tarot should be taken proudly into intellectual as well as theatrical arenas with a positive interpretation for the renewing of the public's mind about this tradition. The Sword can be carried proudly, turning those projections into fluid forms and energy patterns which can support Tarot's new growth and new world of acclaim, which is just now opening out. Now is the time to take up the Sword and plan the next step in individual and collective strategy for the future. May Tarot divination bring the vision for the next step, and may the Sword be taken up with great pride and courage to execute it.

NOTES

1. A. E. Waite, *The Holy Grail* (New York: University Books, 1961), pp. 572–574 ff. Robert V. O'Neill, *Tarot Symbolism* (Lima, OH: Fairway Press, 1986), p. 87. William G. Gray, "The Four Magical Instruments," in Basil Wilby, ed., *The New Dimensions Red Book* (Cheltenham, England: Helio Book Service Ltd., 1968), pp. 41–44.

2. Marie-Louise Sjoestedt, *Gods and Heroes of the Celts* (Berkeley, CA: Turtle Island Foundation, 1982), p. 18. Jessie Weston, *From Ritual to Romance* (New York: Anchor Books, 1957), p. 66.

3. Francis King and Stephen Skinner, *Techniques of High Magic* (New York: Destiny Books, 1976), pp. 60–61.

4. Joseph Maxwell, *The Tarot* (New York: Samuel Weiser, 1977), pp. 139–140.

5. Stuart R. Kaplan, *Tarot Cards for Fun and Fortune Telling* (New York: U.S. Games Systems, 1970), p. 61.

6. Joseph Campbell and Richard Roberts, *Tarot Revelations* (San Francisco: Richard Roberts, 1979), pp. 9–11.

7. Juliet Sharman-Burke, *The Complete Book of Tarot* (New York: St. Martin's Press, 1985), pp. 45–46.

8. James Hillman, "On the Necessity of Abnormal Psychology: Ananke and Athene," in James Hillman, ed., *Facing the Gods* (Dallas: Spring Publications, 19––), pp. 18–27.

Attributions of the Five Universal Shapes

Five Universal Shapes Found in All Art	Universal Meanings Attributed to the 5 Shapes	Four Power Ways in Medicine Wheels	Universal Meditation Practices	Tarot Symbols That Relate to the 5 Shapes & Medicine Wheel
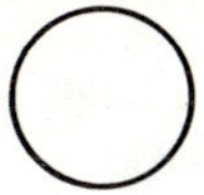	Individuation Independence Wholeness	Way of Warrior/ Leader	Standing Meditation	Adjustment/Justice Chariot Emperor Lust/Strength Magician
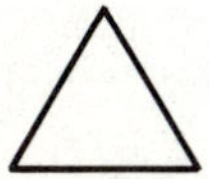	Envisioning Planning Seeking	Way of Visionary	Walking Meditation	High Priestess Hermit Fool Pan/Devil
	Stability Solidity Security	Four-fold Pattern: 4 Elements 4 Directions 4 Seasons	Silence	Four Universal Energies: —Sun —Moon —Star —Universe
	Relationship Integration Synthesis	Way of Healer	Lying Meditation	Empress Tower Art/Temperance Lovers
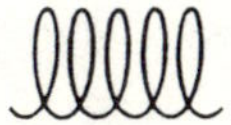	Growth Evolution Change	Way of Teacher	Sitting Meditation	Hierophant Death Hanged Man Aeon/Judgement

ANGELES ARRIEN

The Tarot Renaissance: Ancient Imagery for Contemporary Use

NINETEEN SIXTY-EIGHT WAS THE BEGINNING of my journey with Tarot, and during that time it's been exciting to see how Tarot has been applied in many diverse areas, particularly since 1978. That year, at the California Institute of Integral Studies in San Francisco, an accredited graduate school that offers M.A. and Ph.D. degrees in comparative philosophy, religion, psychology, and social and cultural anthropology, something happened which began to bring Tarot out of the closet and make it a self-help tool. This was that it was offered for credit. Tarot was put into an arena in which psychologists and therapists could begin to use it as a visual affirmation tool. It was lifted out of its prior historical reputation, which began in the middle ages, when it was put into card form to be used for fortune telling. Tarot now became a way of developing and increasing our access to intuition, honoring the intuitive reservoirs we all have within us, what native cultures call the four ways of seeing: vision, intuition, perception, and insight.

One of my questions in 1978 was why the I-Ching, the Oriental book of changes, has so much more credibility than Tarot. The I-Ching, based on nature metaphors, is a book of wisdom, and the Tarot itself is a book of wisdom. The Major Arcana ties in beautifully with the major archetypes or base symbols that belong to collective experience, which each one of us at different times in our lives is aware of when a cluster of symbols come together and are experienced as a theme in our life temporarily, or for some people, for years.

I thought it was exciting that Tarot was now being used to train young professionals, particularly therapists, philosophers, and people exploring spiritual practices, religion, and social and cultural anthropology. I also became rather excited that there was a new forum in which people from different professions could come together—people working with symbols, such as imagery in advertising, healing, business, literature, religion, and philosophy; imagery among the native peoples of the world. There is no place on this planet where imagery in symbols is not used. This led me into a seven-year study that began with wondering whether the same shapes are found in all art globally. That was followed by my second question: If the same shapes are found in all art, what does that say about the human psyche that produces those same shapes in all the cultures of the world? I finally uncovered the notion that there are five shapes found globally in all art. Those five shapes are the circle, the square, the triangle, the spiral, and the equidistant cross, also known as the plus sign.

I'd like you to stop here for a moment and number your preferences for those five shapes. This is a preferential diagnostic tool that I've designed as a result of my cross-cultural work. Note your most preferred shape as one and your least preferred shape as five. By noting at this moment which has more resistance and which has least resistance for you, you will be able to experience the universal process that's taking place in you right now.

In numbering these five universal shapes and noting which shapes begin to vie for position, you may have a couple that seem to be in position number two, or a couple that come up in position number one, while you're pushing them to the bottom for position number five.

Here are the meanings of the positions: Position one is the process that currently has your attention. So whichever of the five shapes—circle, cross, square, triangle, or spiral—you have in position one represents where you think you are or where you want to be. It's currently a source of inspiration.

On the other hand, position five is a process about which you still have some judgment to make, or have experienced in so much depth that you want to put it on the back burner. Maybe you can't quite tolerate it, or it may be a process that you've outgrown.

Position three is a process occurring in your nature that you may be overlooking because position one has your attention. It is the process that, if you will attend to it, is the source of unlimited creativity, healing, and the ability to face the changes you're currently going through. It is the place where the major archetypes, or major symbols, are working within your nature. If you will attend to that, there will be unlimited creativity to handle your current transition.

Position two is your inherent strength, whether you are conscious of it or not. It's that part of you that works effortlessly. It's the process that other people witness in you and always give you feedback on.

Position four was the hidden task or challenge that provoked or ignited you to move to where you are now. In Oriental philosophy this is referred to as "the ox-hurting poke." It was the test that brought you to position three, where you currently are, whether you are aware of it or not.

After I uncovered the fact that there are five shapes found in all art, and that they are these five shapes, then I went back into mythology and folklore, and also into the psychological and spiritual practices of different cultures, to find the meanings most attributed to these shapes. It was astounding to me to discover that ninety-five percent of the cultures agree on the meanings of these shapes! What we have here are really five universal processes of healing, of spiritual growth and evolution, or five universal processes that support people's creative work. Regardless of cultural conditioning or family imprinting, these are the five shapes that were brought into art, and they are associated with five universal processes that we want to express.

The circle is the process of individuation. The majority of cultures see this shape as standing for individuation, independence, totality, and wholeness. There are two major themesongs to this shape: "I've got to be me," and "Don't fence me in." Any position where you have the circle is a place where the underlying need is for space, and space is equated with love and trust. The more space you give a person, the more they will be there; the less space you give a person who's in an individuation process, the more they'll feel unloved and untrusted, and therefore move away. You can always find whether someone is in an individuation cycle: all you have to do is ask them, "What time will you be home tonight?" Anyone who's in a strong individuation process will say, "Well, somewhere between six and eleven." Notice all the leeway they give themselves. Or they'll say, "You'll see me when you see me." The underlying need is the need for space. The more space they're given, the more they'll be around; the less space they're given, the more space they'll take. The underlying fear of anyone who's in a circle process is the fear of entrapment, of being limited, restricted, or restrained. Taken to the extreme, this is the process of narcissism—being so self-absorbed they can't connect with other people. In all myths, cross-culturally, we have the journey of the hero and the journey of the heroine, and that whole myth is a circle at work. Every journey of the hero and the heroine is for the purpose of individuation, independence, becoming more whole, coming into their own totality.

Another universal shape is the equidistant cross, or plus sign. Universally this is not seen as a religious symbol—only in the West. It is a consistent shape in all cultures. It's associated with the process of relationship or relatedness, and with interface, intersection, integration, and synthesis. Buckminster Fuller called this the "synergistic principle," the bringing together of two or more things that create a whole greater than the sum of their parts. Anyone in a relatedness process has an underlying need for quality of time shared. For them, love and trust are equated with time shared. This person asks the question, "What time are you going to be home tonight?" These are people who want to connect, join, integrate ideas, projects, and situations to create a greater whole. These are people who love teamwork and collaborative effort. Their underlying fear is the fear of loss or abandonment. Taken to the extreme, it is the loss of identity, or living only through another person's life or project. These are people who will say, "If you cared about me, you would have called to tell me that you'd be late." They will say things like, "You know, I think there should be one night a week that is our time together." Or, "I think it would be wonderful to get a team of four people together and work on this project for the next three months." It's quality time shared.

In all mythology, you have what's called the journey of the twins, which again is the relatedness process: stories like "Hansel and Gretel," or America's journey of the twins, "Raggedy Ann and Raggedy Andy." Stories about the prince and the pauper, two brothers, or two sisters, are all the shared journey, the journey of the twins. I love Scott Peck's definition of love. He says that love is the capacity to support the spiritual growth and evolution of another human being in equal proportion to one's own spiritual growth and development.

So with these five spiritual processes, if we can honor and support the process a person is in, instead of taking things personally, then we can contribute to their growth and development. Most often with couples the issue about time and space needs to be negotiated. These are issues of the circle and the cross. Both people should have their needs met.

The square, cross-culturally, is associated with foundation setting, stability, solidity, and security. It's very interesting that in the West, the square often appears in positions four or five. But in eastern countries and also in Shamanic places, the square comes up most often in positions one and two, and quite often in position three. In Jungian psychology, if you dream about a cluster of four—say, four people or four cities or four animals—four is associated with something becoming whole or being secured or stabilized within the psyche. With the shamanic societies, in the journey to the lower world, if an animal appears to you four times, it becomes your power animal. If a teacher appears four times in a journey to the upper world, he or she becomes your inner teacher or your inner guide. So the square is associated with something being stabilized and solidified. People in this process have a need for responsibility, accountability, consistency, and congruity. It would be very hard for people who are in square processes to handle double messages, or to handle irresponsibility, inconsistencies, or incongruities. These are the people who come to meetings and say, "What's on our agenda?" These are people who ask, "Who's going to be responsible for this task?"

Children, for example, have the square in positions one or two until they're seven or eight years old. Children often say, "But you broke your promise, you broke your promise again." They want consistency, congruity. The square is the congruity, the alignment between actions and words. Therefore it's associated with integrity and honesty. Here, actions are associated with love and trust. Anyone who is in a square process is going to look to actions. They will say, "If you really cared about me, you would have done what you said you were going to do." The underlying fear for someone in the square process is the fear that nothing's ever going to be done or accomplished, that it's all going to be a waste of time, and they'll never see tangible results. These are people who talk about ideas for a long time. They want to see if the ideas are workable, how they can be implemented. Taken to the extreme, this is a process of rigidity and compulsiveness.

In mythology all cultures have what's called the four-fold way, which is aspects of four coming together—four tests, four seasons, four Gospels, or the four noble truths. Any combination of four is associated with the square—something wanting to be stabilized and secured.

The triangle is associated with vision; it's the searcher, the seeker, the visionary, the planner. Nature's triangle is the mountain. Humankind's imitation of the mountain is the pyramid or the arrowhead; it's a vision where you can see your goal. Triangle process people are very good at one-year plans or five-year plans; they can see what's needed and what's not working, and they can take the organization or the family or the relationship to the next step. The need here is for shared vision. Shared vision is equated with love and trust. These are people who say things like, "Can't you see the possibility of the impact Tarot is going to make on this culture in the next five years?" And if somebody says, "No, I don't get it," these people feel unloved and untrusted, because they are the visionaries and they can see potential. They have the inventive, futuristic minds. Their underlying fear is that there will be no more dreams, no more goals, no more visions. Taken to the extreme, people in this process live so much in the future that they aren't very productive in the present. They seldom get things done because they are so involved in the goal or the vision. All cultures have what are known as vision quests, or the wanderer myth, or the quest for the Grail. Most cultures have a King Arthur and the knights of the round table story. They don't all call it King Arthur, but it's the same visionary quest. It's a spiritual journey as well. It's our own life purpose, our life goals, in that triangle. All cultures have sacred mountains. The tie between mountains and the triangle and spirituality and vision is interesting. There is a very strong cultural imprinting globally.

Then we have the spiral. In art this symbol is found spiraling upward or spiraling downward, or is shown as flat within itself. In most cultures this is seen as the process of growth and evolution. It's the need for variety, the need for change and flexibility. In the spiral process, flexibility is equated with love and trust. The more flexible you are with the person who needs variety in their life, the more they are going to feel loved and trusted. The less flexible you are about their needs for variety, the more they are going to feel unloved and untrusted. Their underlying fear is that things are going to be too boring, too routine, too predictable. That's a huge fear for someone in a spiral process. If they feel that work is going to be boring, or that their relationship is becoming predictable, they will create change just to keep variety in it. Taken to the extreme, this is the process of the dilettante, someone who delights in many things but cannot explore any of them in depth.

All cultures have spinning stories and weaving stories. These stories are literally about growth and evolution, stories about people's needs for variety and change. And there are also stories about coming back to a similar situation, with the same people playing the parts, but somehow coming at it from a different level of awareness—the spiral—seeing it through different eyes. The Greek myth of Ariadne is certainly a story associated with the spiral. All the Native American trickster stories in which the trickster figure promotes change in people's lives, change that supports growth in evolution; the spider woman stories: all these are associated with the spiral.

Interestingly, a Persian poet by the name of Rumi said, "Beyond ideas of wrongdoing and rightdoing, there is a field; I'll meet you there." Position one is our current idea of rightdoing, and position five is our current idea of wrongdoing. Position one also represents the future. Position five represents the past. And position three is the present work to be done. Position two is your inherent strength, which could assist you now in supporting position three. And position four is the challenge that ignited or pushed you into position three, where you are now—it was literally the motivating factor that pushed you to grow to where you are now.

Position three represents the new life within your nature. By attending to it, you can unleash unlimited creativity and healing, the ability to support your current transition, if you will just move from the mesmerization of position one and focus on the work to be done in the present.

All cultures have salvation myths and doomsday myths. A few years ago I realized that if that's so, then we must have some bridging myths as well. Perhaps we've been overlooking the bridging myths as much as we've been overlooking position three. I found that there is indeed a whole body of such myths, and they could collapse salvation-doomsday polarities. These are myths that come up during times of change, whether personal, professional, spiritual, global, or cultural. In times of change we move to our favorite salvation myth, perhaps of being a Pollyanna, or thinking about the Second Coming of the Messiah or UFOs.

Position one is our current salvation myth. If we don't move into that polarity of salvation during times of change, then we move into the other polarity, which is doomsday. These are the classic myths of Armageddon, the Apocalypse, the end of the world—nuclear war, nuclear winter. Our current doomsday myth is position five.

Every culture has creation myths. And what are creation myths but stories about how to build new worlds internally and externally. That's a whole body of myths that have been overlooked. Yet the next twenty years will require us to begin to tap techniques of creative problem-solving and transcend polarities of salvation and doomsday, so that we can build new worlds internally and externally.

Position three is our current creation myth. That's where we can build new worlds internally and externally. It's where we can collapse salvation or doomsday. You can collapse the developmental tension—the paradoxes or polarities in your own nature—and create a synergistic principle by bringing two or more things together to make a greater whole.

In 1978 I established the International Tarot Symposium in San Francisco as a forum where people could come together and share thoughts about Tarot. And we found that people have been applying Tarot in many innovative ways. Tarot has been used in jails to assist prisoners. It has been used in the business world to facilitate personnel issues. There are students who have worked with Tarot in corporations such as large medical groups, food companies, and solar heating companies. They have taken Tarot into therapy, into the healing arts, and into education, working with children. They are beginning to demystify Tarot and to show that it is the "western book of changes," just as the I-Ching is the eastern book of changes. Among corporate logos, all of the five shapes occur. You might take a look at your own business cards and see which shapes are prevalent, or look at your company brochures. Notice what universal processes you are supporting in your work. Wherever I need space in my life, the circle is working. Wherever I am planning and envisioning new goals and directions for myself, the triangle is working. Wherever I need to share my journey and work collaboratively, the cross is working. Wherever I want things to be tangible, applicable, and consistent, the square is working in my life; and where I need variety, the spiral is at work.

Consistently, in all cultures the circle becomes the container for many shapes. In the East we call this the mandala, a Sanskrit word meaning "that which is of the essence." The circle contains that which is the essence. In Africa they refer to the circle as the gratitude hoop. Among Asian societies, groups of people who meet in a circle for counseling work are called "the singing bamboo reed—where people shall be firm yet yielding." Among Native American people the circle is called the medicine wheel.

You can also view the Major Arcana as a medicine wheel. The circle is the process of individuation and wholeness. Native people say that life can be very simple if we follow the four-fold way. This four-fold way has some principles also used in Alcoholics Anonymous. Life would be simple if, one, we show up; two, we pay attention; three, we tell the truth without blame or judgment; and four, we remain unattached to the outcome and open to the outcome.

In the Native American medicine wheel, the Oriental singing bamboo reed, the African gratitude hoop, and the mandala, which are all metaphors for the circle, the four-fold pattern supports the circle. So underneath every circle is also the square, the four directions, the four-fold way, which makes things stable and solid and secure.

In native traditions the north is associated with the way of the warrior; the south is associated with the way of the healer; the east is the way of the visionary; and the west is the way of the teacher. These are what's known as the four-fold way. My most recent research has been a study of the four ways of expression in the world by the majority of cultures. Interestingly enough, the process of individuation or wholeness involves these four ways, the ways of the warrior, the healer, the visionary, and the teacher.

These four ways are found in all mythology and within the Major Arcana. If you think about your favorite Major Arcana cards right now, and your least favorite, this will tell you what needs to be developed in your own nature. Many of us may have a well-developed healer, teacher, and visionary, but an under-developed warrior. And many of us may have a well-developed warrior-healer combination, but an undeveloped healer-teacher combination.

These four ways also tie in with the four suits of the Minor Arcana. The Swords are the north, the warrior. The Cups are associated with the south, primarily because healing comes through the expression of love and love is a quality of the south. Wands are the way of the visionary, the east. Wands are a suit associated with spirituality and intuition—the core of who we are and what's going on in our deep internal natures. And Pentacles are associated with the way of the teacher, the west (our bodies are incredible teachers). Also, the west is the place of letting go and not being attached to outcomes. Death is our teacher of detachment.

The way of the warrior is the home of the three powers—the power of presence, the power of communication, and the power of your willingness to take a stand. These are the three kinds of power that come up over and over again. The Emperor is very much a warrior, a symbol of power and leadership, and a way of increasing your ability to empower yourself and others. The Strength card is also a warrior. It requires the ability to know what your passions, limits, and boundaries are. The Strength card is the beauty—your gifts—that has tamed the beast within you. It's only by accessing your inner warrior that you can tame the beast within, rather than allow it to tame you. This requires you, whether male or female, to tap into your receptivity and be willing to receive your divine inheritance, your gifts, talents, and resources. Jung calls this receptivity the anima.

The Chariot also falls into the category of the warrior. It's the only archetype in the deck that combines quietude with activity, or stillness with movement. The contemplative reposed figure is also the readied charioteer. This is the universal meaning of warrior, especially in the martial arts, such as Aikido and Tai Chi, that one must be firm yet yielding. The Chariot teaches us to have movement and quietude equally in our life—an important quality of the inner warrior.

The Justice card, the woman who stands in the diamond, piercing veils of illusion, delusion, and deception, definitely embodies the way of the warrior. The commitment to be an inner warrior is to pierce those veils. It's the warrior aspect of us that tells us right away whether we are in or out of balance or adjustment. It is the warrior within us who wants to rectify matters, be fair and just. Also, with the warrior it's important to recognize that the north in most traditions is a place where we're willing to stand up for ourselves. It's the home of the winged creatures, of father sky; it brings that kind of clarity. And standing meditation is a universal meditation through which we can transform the inner victim, to claim the inner warrior.

The way of the healer is the south—the home of the green meadow, the place of four-legged creatures, and the direction of renewal. It's a place of love, trust, and forgiveness. It's staying open-hearted, clear-hearted, and full-hearted. So, if I have healing work to do with my relations, the south is the place to go. The south is also the home of the drum, and the drum is humankind's imitation of the heartbeat. The way of the healer encompasses the Empress. Love with wisdom, love that doesn't push or hold back, requires a heart that is trusting, rather than controlling.

The way of the healer is the home of the Tower, a major symbol of renovation and restoration. Healing also includes the need to destructure whatever is not working in our lives, or that we've outgrown, so we can begin to renovate or restore that which is actual and true.

The Temperance card is in the south. It is the place where we "temper" ourselves. In the Crowley deck it's the art card, which is the principle of integration and synthesis. Temperance and integration are healing modes. And, of course, the Lovers card is also within the way of the healer. Appreciation, validation, recognition, gratitude, and interest are the arms of love. The Lovers is the major archetype that teaches us about the universal kinds of love—love between parent and child, between colleagues, between mates, between lovers—passionate love, unconditional love, spiritual love, and the love of self.

The east is the way of the visionary. It is the place of singing for your life, the place of truth and authenticity. Cross-culturally, it is a place of unlimited creativity, your life purpose, your life vision, your life dream, and actualizing all that. In Tarot, a primary access to the visionary within you, especially in the Major Arcana, is through the High Priestess.

As we've noted, the four ways of seeing are vision, insight, perception, and intuition. The Hermit's vision comes from contemplation and introspection. The Fool is a visionary. To the extent that the Fool is courage, this is the willingness to stand behind whatever has meaning in your life. The Fool stands for curiosity, child-like wonder, innocence, and freshness, and the capacity to give birth to new forms, to experience no fear. The Fool represents fearlessness in applying your vision.

The Devil card, also known as the Pan card, is the way of the visionary, primarily because, until the middle ages, this card was the archetype of Pan, and Bacchus and Dionysus. It's the only card in the deck that combines mirth with practicality. It's the merry goat, revealing that the true evil in life is really not implementing your life's dream. Your own bedevilment is not living your life vision. I look at where I'm too serious, to see where I'm attached. Seriousness teaches about attachment. By contrast, wherever I maintain my sense of humor, I can implement my vision and not take things so seriously. This is mirth and practicality, the merry earth goat, Pan, Bacchus.

And then there is the way of the teacher, the west. It's the place of letting go, the place of not being attached to outcomes. It's learning how to be comfortable with not knowing. In the west it's the home of the ancestor spirits, of grandmother ocean, the water creatures, the great mystery of who you are. In the way of the teacher is the Hierophant, the inner teacher. Spiritual learnings, being in touch with deep wisdom. The way of the teacher also includes the Death card, the teacher of attachments and letting go, the ancestor spirits. And the Hanged Man is here also, teaching you about breaking patterns that bind, limit, and restrict you from your freedom. Here also is the Judgement card, the place of using good judgment, transforming the judge to the fair witness, being comfortable with not knowing. Good judgment rather than critical judgment is the ideal.

The medicine wheel itself is supported by three natural organic entities. The sun shines on every medicine wheel and is the symbol of universal dynamism. The moon, which shines on every medicine wheel, is the symbol of universal magnetism, the magnetic pull. The Star or stars are associated with the third universal energy to draw upon, which is the principle of integration. Dynamism, magnetism, and integration are the three universal life forces, the three kinds of light—the strong light of the sun, the soft light of the moon, and the integrated light of the stars. We ourselves are walking stars, medicine wheels on a giant star, and that giant star is earth, or the Universe card. When you look at the kinds of light in the heavens they remind you of the life forces within—the sun, dynamism; the moon, magnetism; the star, integration. It is our purpose to bring dynamism, magnetism, and integration to this planet, to our universe, the world, Mother Earth. In Antonio Muchado's poem, "To Healing," a quatrain that comes from a longer poem is fitting here. When we work with the Major Arcana as a medicine wheel, and the five universal shapes found in all art, we might very well have this experience:

> I dreamt last night,
> Oh marvelous error,
> That honeybees were in my heart
> Making honey out of my old failures.

EILEEN CONNOLLY

Pathways to Understand the Major Arcana: Preview of the Upcoming Connolly Deck

I HAVE WAITED ANXIOUSLY FOR FORTY YEARS TO see the beginning of the New Age. Each decade I waited for it to happen. It began slowly and has continued at a steady pace throughout the years. As each new and exciting method of divination was exposed, as each new theory was expressed, growth became rapid and evident. But while the New Age was growing, it was also stunted through lack of basic detail and knowledge. No new and exciting theories were being introduced. Repetition was a culprit, along with lack of understanding and the inability to delve into what already existed. As each new generation of metaphysicians came along with its own individual approach, there was still the same general subject matter. Only a few exceptional human beings contributed their knowledge and experience for the benefit of all.

Fortunately, some of the pioneers wrote books. Even today, the well-rounded student uses these works. In recent years, I feel that the roots of the New Age have been established firmly, perhaps for the first time. It is actually happening now. You are a part of it. Let yourself feel the excitement of these vital days. Your contribution is your participation. Whatever you learn will become a part of your personal foundation. From these seeds you will participate and express your esoteric vocations.

Why have we waited so long? The answer is simple. Growth and study are the results of good teaching. New teachers are beginning to emerge as a result of study, and the students are seeking answers at last. Not necessarily from the teaching of new theories, but from dedicated teachers who have contributed and expanded upon the original theories based on the universal concepts. The universe and its secrets have been veiled for too long. Contemporary attitudes and present-day thinking demand and expect answers. You can look around and see how by thrusting forward, many scholars have presented the world with some of these answers.

Continuous pursuit of knowledge and how to make it work on an everyday basis is now bringing us closer to the realization and reality of the New Age. Scholarly discoveries and practices are now opening esoteric doors of self-exploration. Only by the traditional method of teaching and developing can the New Age hope to continue its forward movement. We must share. That is just one of the keys. Secrets of ancient tradition are now being released to responsible students. One thing is true: When the student is ready, the master appears. Many of these secrets contain the answers to present-day situations. The need for secrecy is not always applicable in today's world, except of course, if comprehension is not possible. The masters are now opening all levels of consciousness to enable the seeking student to understand the ancient mysteries and make them applicable to today.

Simplicity is one of the ancient keys to Tarot. It is a well-established fact that mere exposure to the Tarot and its images immediately alerts a higher level of consciousness. Any difficulty noted is not in comprehending the symbols, but rather the higher self's seeming inability to transfer knowledge to the conscious mind. Because of progress—civilization, if you will—the everyday conscious level has little or no patience. All answers, interpretations, and reasoning have to be spontaneous, quick and easy to understand. Our contemporary mode of life not only teaches immediate intellectual response, but demands it. The ancient philosophers, sages, and scholars did not have this constant need to respond instantly and correctly. Lifestyles then included time to really think, to open the doors into the subconscious and the higher consciousness, and allow wisdom to flow. Now we call this form of thought meditation.

As many good teachers know, meditation time must be allowed for the student to simply look at the Tarot cards. During this apparently non-productive period, the exposure to Tarot symbolism will, in itself, provide the correct source of interpretation. This can be proven quite easily. Whenever you have difficulty analyzing a spread, just relax and let your esoteric mechanism work. In much the same way, you get into your car and drive and are not in the least concerned with what is taking place mechanically; you just know it works.

Thoughts are living things. We allow ourselves to think and then judge whether or not we should act accordingly. Anything we do begins with one thought. We think about going somewhere and decide then to put our thought into action.

It is not difficult to understand why so much mystery surrounds New Age philosophy. One of the many reasons is that mystery is a method of protection. Protection became necessary because of varying levels of fear and abuse in regard to ancient teachings. Throughout time, those interested in esoteric philosophies were open to ridicule. Some were punished unjustly. History has recorded many such actions taken through sheer misunderstanding. This archaic thinking is disappearing, and in the twentieth century the world gradually has become more and more accepting. People with New Age concepts and beliefs are emerging as an intellectual force throughout the world. We can see their growth and development. Young men and women are accepting their esoteric abilities and integrating them as a way of life. Once this attitude is fully accepted, we definitely will be ready to advance forward.

Since I wrote my first book on Tarot quite a few years ago, many more books have been written. At that time, it was questionable whether or not such a book would succeed. I am fortunate that my books have been a success, and this can only be a sign of tremendous growth, of interest and practice by students of Tarot.

When I wrote that first book, I imagined a student, one lonely student, unable to attend a class, unable to find a way to study. I wrote the book to open the world of Tarot to those who were interested and was extremely careful not to assume that my readers had any previous knowledge of the subject. In planning my own new Tarot deck, I had the same concept and motivation that I had when I began to write the first Tarot book for the apprentice—to provide what a serious student might need. I wanted to present a visual picture in a very beautiful way and to eliminate unnecessary symbolism, in order to bring the Tarologist—a word I coined many years ago to define a scholar of Tarot—a closer view. Once the Tarologist recognizes the simple code of the three conscious levels of perfection

—the conscious level, the subconscious level and the higher conscious—we can then allow the internal esoteric interaction between these levels to become activated.

It has been said that all those attracted to the royal road of Tarot have already walked far along the path of life. As long as the Tarologist is sensitive and competent, any negative possibilities that appear will be interpreted with the required level of intellect and counseling ability.

Each of the Minor cards opens a door. The visual image indicates the nature and content of the card. Access to the Connolly symbolism permits the reader a full, rich, detailed interpretation. The Tarologist does not need to struggle on a conscious level. The esoteric interpretations will flow easily into a well-prepared mind. As we all know, a well-balanced reading is only possible when the reader is in good spiritual balance. The Connolly deck becomes a complementary source for the input and sensitivity of the reader.

I personally derive a great deal of pleasure from color. Color represents vibrations. The vibrations of color alert the superconsciousness, and we gain a higher insight through this complex vibratory force. It is an esoteric function: the student, on the conscious level, is provided with the information first instigated by the vibratory structure of color.

The various historic periods of dress for both male and female have always been of great interest to me. In Tarot the Fool has a wardrobe rich in color and historic design, as he travels on his spiritual journey, the path of life. Years ago, one of my earliest memories of visualization, I saw the pictures now being presented in the Connally deck.

Card thirteen of the Major Arcana, the Death card, is often used when there is an occasion to portray some horrific circumstance, be it in a movie or whatever. I am sure that you, yourself, or perhaps someone you read for, has experienced the short intake of breath that this card brings. Let me add that because of the beasts and skeletons portrayed on Tarot cards, and the obvious misunderstanding of the ancient symbolism, which I do not deny, many would-be students have simply been put off by certain aspects of visual interpretation. The Death card in the Connolly deck is referred to as the card of transition. This basically means a total change from one set of circumstances to another. You see a man leaving a dark room. Behind him he has left the bishop's miter and the king's crown which have represented important issues and beliefs in life. Under his feet you see the transition energy taking place. He stands in the archway as a cherub holds the fountain of new healing waters. White roses portray the man's new purity of thought and future intent. He leaves the old behind, he looks out and is overwhelmed by the new beauty and transition before him.

The Major Arcana, which are the original Tarot deck, portray the path of man. The Fool begins the journey and each following card highlights the journey of the soul. As we reach the last card and see the female figure in command, joyous and triumphant, we must remember that it is the victory of the Fool on all three levels of consciousness. Throughout the deck, you will see the three levels of consciousness portrayed as a man on the conscious level, a woman as the subconscious and a child, cherub or angel as the higher consciousness. The various soul experiences of the Fool are seen as he walks the path.

Colors contribute to the understanding and interpretation of the Tarot. The depth and intensity of bright color, along with its pastel shades, allow the Tarologist a completely free emotional expression according to the demands of the situation.

Tarot is the story of life. It has been my whole life. I am not a newcomer to Tarot. At the age of 12, I visited a fair that had come to my town in Great Britain. The fair miraculously transformed the downtown area into a fairyland of lights, with huge terrifying rides, a haunted mansion, and hot black peas. I was absolutely fascinated and felt compelled to walk through the highly colored caravans of the gypsies. All children, especially well-brought-up children, were repeatedly warned by parents to keep away from gypsies. Gypsies were dark and mysterious and traveled with the fairground company, the men and boys helping to erect equipment and the women making wooden clothes pegs and telling fortunes. Some read palms. They would first ask to have their palms crossed with silver. In those days, the least expensive silver coin in Great Britain was a threepenny bit, which I think is approximately three cents. Incidentally, these threepenny bits were also used at Christmas time. Mothers would make the Christmas pudding and drop in threepenny bits wrapped in wax paper. It was considered extremely lucky if your piece of pudding contained a threepenny bit, and to this day, I still make Christmas puddings, but now I put dimes in them.

The gypsy women were also clairvoyants and they read the tea leaves. It was mostly women who went to see the gypsies. At twelve years old, I would stand and watch to see what happened. I wondered what mysterious secrets the gypsies told these women. The women would pay sixpence, which was a lot of money, and an old gypsy would pour dark black tea from a cracked teapot into a thick cup. The cup was then thrust into the hand of the waiting woman, who would sip it nervously, looking around, I suppose, to see if anyone saw her outside the gypsy's tent. When the tea had been drunk, the gypsy would swirl the dregs around the cup and ask the woman to take it in to see Madame Rosita. I never did see Madame Rosita. Behind the gypsy tent stood rows of brightly painted wagons, where dark long-haired children ran around in bare feet, laughing. On the steps of one of these wagons I saw an old, old gypsy. I can still see her face now: it was like leather, tanned with outdoor living. Peeping over the top of a half-door were two little children with dirty faces and big black eyes. The old gypsy wore a long black dress and a tightly wrapped red-and-white-spotted turban. Around her neck she wore a silvery scarf. She wore long hooped earrings and multiple layers of pendants and gold necklaces, rings on her long bony fingers and bangles halfway up her arm. I had never seen a lady dressed like this before.

She was laying out colored cards such as I had also never seen. I was intrigued and curious as I bravely stepped nearer. She looked up and saw me, and beckoned to me. I was frightened. I thought about the stories of gypsies stealing children. I remembered what my mother had said. The old gypsy invited me to sit down. I asked what she was doing. She smiled again and clicked her long dirty fingernails on the cards, telling me that she had been waiting for me. Scooping up the cards with the strange pictures, she gave them to me and asked me to shuffle them. I was certainly no expert and I dropped what I later discovered to be the High Priestess. To this day, I marvel when I think about the things she told me. She said I would be highly educated, that I would teach the world many things about the Tarot. I wanted to know more. She told me that if I brought sandwiches and a little trinket for her, she would tell me what I needed to know, and that that was why we had met.

I can't begin to tell you the many white lies I told my mother during the following week, as I found excuses to visit the grandmother gypsy. While children played and lonely women entered the fortune-telling tents, I listened carefully. I received the foundations and the wisdom for the path of life. I knew it was important to remember. It was imperative that I know more without really knowing why. I knew this lady was a great spiritual teacher and I also knew I was destined to follow a spiritual path.

During that week, I spent as much time as I could listening and learning. It rained continually throughout the week. One day, as the fair was being taken down, the gypsy grandmother told me that I would not see her after that day. I didn't believe it and told her I would study what she had taught me and see her again at the summer fair. She shook her head sadly and said, "My work is finished and I am going." I didn't understand where she was going to.

I never did see her again, but I pursued my new interest. Of course, I did not own a Tarot deck and had no idea where one could be purchased. I resorted to simple line drawings and careful pencil-written notes, knowing even then that one day I would create my own cards. It was many years before I owned my own deck. They were not readily available in those days. I always maintained a deep interest in Tarot and would go to the library to find what I could relating to the subject. I never found a Tarot teacher. I began my serious interest five years after meeting the gypsy lady. And at that time also I began to study the Cabala and other esoteric subjects.

The knowledge I learned as a young girl was verified during my years of Cabalistic studies and research. Through those years, I have continued to be amazed, because I found that the esoteric rudiments the old gypsy had given me were absolute and true Cabalistic theories then not readily available. I have often thought about her during my years of intensive research. I valued the precious time and the wonderful exciting six days when this great lady shared her spiritual wisdom with a little girl named Eileen Holmes, who could give her only a broken pin and a promise that I have kept all my life.

Peter Paul, my youngest son, created the portrayal of the Major Arcana for the Connolly deck, available in 1989. When Peter was six years old, I knew he would be working with me to create this deck. I have given birth to six children—three sons and three daughters—but I knew that Peter would be the one doing this. Peter remembers me telling him that he had been born with exceptional artistic talent and that one day he would help me to produce my Tarot deck. I have waited patiently for many years.

Without a doubt he developed an unusual ability in art. During his high-school years, I saw a style develop. Incidentally, during these growing years, I seldom mentioned the Tarot deck. After graduation, Peter began to paint, and soon his work was accepted in a couple of galleries. That was an exciting time. He obviously had a deep affinity for the 1950s. This was evident in his work hanging on the gallery walls. His work sold, and the images I had carried for many years seemed destined to remain where they were.

But eventually, Peter and I discussed the Connolly deck. I was excited. He was ready, and began to experiment with style. The first four

THE FOOL

paintings were in acrylics. The next four were painted in water colors. He then experimented for the first time with a medium new to him, colored pencils—and went on to produce a magnificent deck with them. The hours he spent are uncountable. His dedication is of the highest. Each card touches the subconscious in a deep and profound way. We have worked closely together to achieve exactly the esoteric interpretations held in my consciousness for so many years. Now I want to introduce and describe in detail the twenty-two Major Arcana of the Connolly deck.

The Fool has climbed the steep cliffs of his higher consciousness from the ocean of his spirituality. We see him poised and in the process of making a choice. Standing on the purple path of the master, his pink and purple tunic denotes strength to make the right choice. On his head he has the golden cap of Kether, with a red feather of individuality. A leather pouch contains his tools, which are the twelve astrological signs, indicating his ability to express himself in all ways. He has no limitations. The white rose of purity is in his left hand, the hand of death. He holds a stout wand with green fertile leaves. His white cuffs will purify his choice. The white dog which represents man waits and watches. The dog's right eye is black. We see that the white dog has a pure intent toward the Fool. Yet the dog as man has a tendency to see another man's choice from a negative point of view. As the Fool begins his journey of life he will experience every level required of man to complete the journey of the soul. The key word for the Fool is Choice.

THE MAGICIAN

THE HIGH PRIESTESS

The Magician has now found the table of life. On his table are the four symbolic tools of life, the Cup, the Wand, the Pentacle, and the Sword. His love and purpose are seen in the beautiful red roses and white lilies that surround him. Dressed in his white gown of purity, he has a green serpent indicating an eternity of accomplishment and learning. Above the Magician's head is the lemniscate—the sign of infinity. The Magician holds a powerful wand in his right hand. He has obviously contributed effort, and the wand glows with spiritual power and ability. His left hand is receiving the light of his skill and manifestation. As above, so below. We are shown conscious application of heavenly energies by the use of free will and spiritual power given to all. The flaring red cloak of individuality protects him as he reaches out and masters the elements over himself and others. The key word for the Magician is Individuality.

The powerful yet gentle femininity of the High Priestess is evident as she sits serenely between the two pillars, representing the positive and negative aspects of life. At her feet is the lunar crescent, glowing with mysterious secrets, partially seen behind the golden gates of Death. She holds the Torah scroll, ready to give to the spiritual seeker. Dressed in a vibrant blue robe of higher and complete spiritual healing and wearing a large gold cross on her breast, she sits on the threshold of our higher consciousness, offering knowledge and wisdom. Behind the golden gates of Death we see the glimmering of a new dawn penetrating our own higher consciousness. This is the sanctuary. Our presence is felt and seen by the

THE EMPRESS

THE EMPEROR

motivation of our higher self. The pool of spirituality by the feet of the High Priestess indicates our need to go beyond the golden gates of Death for wisdom on our life path. The key words are Unseen Wisdom.

The Empress, a regal figure in a vivid pink robe, is seated by a field of ripe growing wheat. To her left is the fountain of life; we see this through the symbology of the butterfly. Before her is a carpet of radiant flowers, and the trees are in full bloom. Fertility and abundance are the magnificent symbols of the Empress. Twelve golden stars encircled by living leaves form the crown on her head. She gives power from her pink-gloved hand, as she holds her scepter mounted with a golden globe that represents this world. On her breast she wears the golden symbol of Venus. The Empress represents the Yin and Yang principles, the Earth Mother, both male and female. She represents fulfillment in all human things. The Empress stands for total balance and makes possible all things as she sits waiting for us to enter her beautiful garden. The key word for the Empress is Abundance.

The Emperor represents power, command, and authority. Dressed in rich, jeweled green robes, his decisions are based on solid foundations. His individuality is firm, yet he does not allow free expression to govern his need for discipline. We see his individuality in the dark red stockings. He is the intellect. Law and order are the roots of his kingdom. His decisions appear to come without emotion. Control is the key to the Emperor as he sits on his throne, firm and reliable. We see the first sign of spring in the pink-tipped crocus behind his throne. He is patient and plans well. In

his left hand he holds the globe; in his right hand, the scepter. Surrounded by spiritual intention, he rules, unswaying and disciplined. With his concept of mind over matter and goals firmly rooted, his is perhaps the brightest vision of all. The key word is Discipline.

The Hierophant is sometimes known as the Pope. He represents external religion and tradition. In his left hand he holds a triple-cross scepter, and with his right hand he gives a blessing. Crossed keys and the dove of the Holy Spirit are to his upper left and right. Standing before a glorious stained-glass window, he traditionally understands all the ways of men. Before him are two young men. One is dressed traditionally and has a focused, attentive gaze. The second young man holds a book. He is a sceptic—not so easily persuaded. The High Priestess waits for us to speak when we are ready to obey our higher consciousness. The Hierophant speaks regardless to all who will listen. The contrast is between tradition and blind acceptance without application of self-thought, as opposed to the new High Priestess, who waits for those who have undergone the self-initiation of spirituality and are ready. Tradition is the key word.

The Lovers. A striking red sun is shown at the top of the card. It is the source of spiritual energy focused in the center. The tree of life is heavily laden with fruit. All levels of consciousness are portrayed. Man is the conscious level. He holds a brightly colored bird on his right hand. The man is seeking answers. Clothed in green for tranquility, he gazes confidently at the female, who is the subconscious level. Her flowing lilac veil is gradually changing to the master color purple as she listens to the joy

THE CHARIOT

STRENGTH

and wisom conveyed by the cherub of higher consciousness from the great angel Raphael overhead. The sky, mountains, and water reflect all levels of consciousness in the act of merging, going directly to the source and maintaining harmony. The key words are Choice with Harmony.

The Chariot. A warrior-hero riding home after his conquest is triumphant and victorious. But look at his eyes: they are full of pain as he leaves behind him the aftermath of battle. Still holding the reins of his chariot, he maintains full control. To his right we see his banner of achievement, blue with spirituality and the stars a bright white, showing a deep level of understanding. The temple of truth stands solidly in the background, untouched by the scars of battle and personal conquest. The warrior has learned to control the forces of the two sphinxes. He can now positively direct each of these two forces. On the front of his chariot is the flying spear of the Egyptian. He now has wisdom and knows the secret of inner knowledge and can use his talents and energy constructively. The key word for the Chariot is Control.

The Strength card shows a young woman with flowers in her hair and in her hand. She peacefully contemplates the beauty around her. Her gentleness merges equally with the strength of the lion. Sitting by her pool of spirituality, the lemniscate is bright above her head, denoting her level of attainment. The clouds are tinged with the pink of power, and in her garden of discipline and tranquility, she shows a love that touches all things. Her power enables her to overcome obstacles. She quietly displays

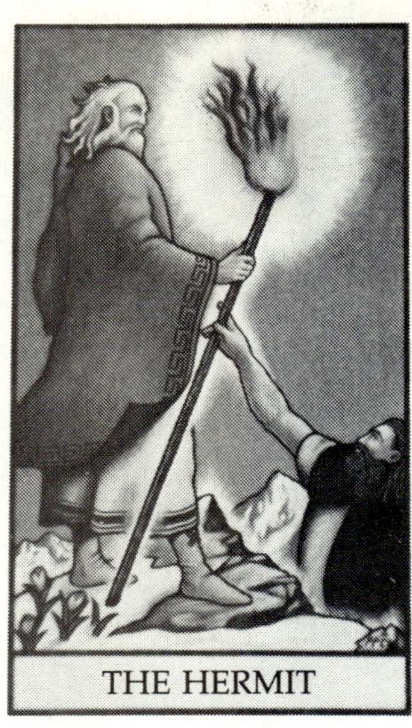

THE HERMIT

WHEEL OF FORTUNE

her strength with inner confidence. Her golden robe portrays her level of spirituality and inner strength. She has no fear and does not feel the need to defend herself. It is the strength of God that permeates the unspoken dignity of this maiden. Higher forces protect all those who submit their fears to God. The key word is Strength.

As we look at the faces of the two men in the Hermit card, we see that the older man is the young man who now knows himself. The Hermit is the higher consciousness that waits at the peak of our own spirituality. Only by thrusting forward purposefully can we hope to make contact with our original staff of life. When the Fool began his journey, the staff was alive with green leaves. Now with the Hermit, a new living force will illuminate the original staff to enable us to continue on the path of life. The younger man, the conscious level, reaches out, and the higher self of wisdom ignites the staff. We see the flame of a higher power lighting up the younger man's subconscious. We see the young man, after the effort of his long climb, now rejoicing as he makes contact with his inner wisdom. Continued desire motivates him to discover the peaks of his higher consciousness. As the flame grows brighter we are given the vision to see our purpose and reach our earthly goals. The key words are Inner Wisdom.

The inscription around the Wheel, translated from the Latin, is, "I reign, I reigned, I am without reign, I shall reign." The four corners of the card show the four original tools of the Magician's table. Use or misuse of

these tools determines our place on the Wheel of Life. Reading clockwise we can see the letters on the wheel: "T A R O." We also see the Hebrew letters which translate to one of the holy names of God. The angel observes man as he balances the Wheel, waiting to give guidance when called upon. The man at the bottom of the Wheel appears amazed and confused. Dressed in his garment of individuality, he sees the tools of the Magician, free and waiting to be used correctly. When man is at the bottom of the Wheel, there is only one way to go and that is up. The Wheel of Life is forever turning. Nothing remains constant. It requires effort to stay at the top and more effort to go back up to the top. As the Wheel constantly turns, man must realize the rhythm and nature of his own Wheel. The key word is Change.

Justice is a strong woman about to reach the top of the steps. Standing between the two pillars, she is dressed in the deep red of individuality. Her need to know and recognize her roots and foundations is seen in her deep green cape. A banner of deep blue and gold falls around her dress, denoting true spirituality and justice. Behind her is the force of earth power that has given her cause to provide justice. In her left hand we see her scales. As the feather falls, the scales are balanced. In her right hand she holds the sword which still reflects the pink tones of earth power and use. Her sword is to the right, the action of man. Her scales are to the left, denoting perfect spiritual balance. Red and white roses remind us that

true justice is given in purity and love. The double-edged sword is symbolic of justice, assuring us that both sides are equally evaluated. The law of karma comes into effect: We reap what we sow. The key words are Justice and Decision.

A young man with a halo of gold and a look of contentment on his face hangs from a living tree. Clothed in varying shades of blue, the Hanged Man obviously has a deep sense of his own spirituality. His shoes, tunic and belt are the vivid red of individuality. He draws energies from the living wood. An air of self-satisfaction surrounds him. The cherub brings to his attention that the ropes are not tied. He brings wisdom to the Hanged Man and advises him that the time to act is now. We sense a reluctance. All is not what it seems. Much is going on behind the scenes. Perhaps he is planning. Perhaps he prefers that those around him see him as being unable to help himself. We must take a closer look at the Hanged Man before we reach conclusions. The key word is Release.

Transition, known as the Death card, is transformation, total change on one's life path. We see the man in the center of his mystical experience, emerging from darkness into light. His robe is green, representing his foundations and roots. Over his robe he wears the protective and generous cloak of purple. His spiritual master has protected his transition and brought him to the light of beneficial change. Under his feet we see the vibratory power of transition. Behind him is the bishop's miter and the

TEMPERANCE

MATERIALISM

golden crown. These are symbolic of his past beliefs and possessions. They are left behind in the dark. His higher consciousness, portrayed by the cherub, is offering him contact with his subconscious. The man points in wonder at the two towers ahead, with the brilliant golden sun beckoning him to new and wonderful opportunities. The white roses of purity indicate that as he gazes in childlike wonder, his future intent is now being purified by his acceptance of transition. The key words are Total Change.

Temperance unites the female and male principles. It is the bringing together of spirit and matter. The inner eye has been awakened by the absorbing power surrounding her head. The force of this transformation, the perfect balance of man and spirituality, causes the red cloak of individuality to fall away. Through love she has been given a new cloak of vision that will penetrate her new consciousness. The bright sun shines, lighting up the dark unexplored areas of the higher consciousness. The Kether crown is impregnated in the sun, caused by the impact of perfect inner control. Gifted with patience and the ability to see things as they really are, Temperance is the key to true joy and harmony. It is acceptance of what is, vision of what could be and the patience to nourish a new and growing spirituality. The key words are Patience and Moderation.

Materialism, normally known as the Devil, shows how the tools of life have been abused. The sturdy wand no longer has the fertile leaves. Through stress and error, man has broken his staff of life. The sword is bent with constant emotional use. His cup is empty, and the grip of the

pentacle appears firm. The man is amazed and wonders how it all happened. But a light of understanding pierces the fog of his dilemma. The chains are not permanent, nor are they secured tightly. His outer garment is a shadowed red of misused individuality. Around his waist is the dark wrap of emotional paralysis. In the background the woman, who is the subconscious, is gazing at the brilliant rainbow, indicating a new dawn of consciousness. The man can release himself immediately. When he accepts and recognizes the source of his own dilemma, he can then remove the costly chains of material attachment. The key word is Materialism.

The Tower shows lightning as a cosmic force that breaks down the false structure and ideals. It originates from the same source that created the Hermit's flame. It is the same power that the Magician uses. As we look at the Tower, we see the doves of the Holy Spirit. One remains to rebuild the Tower and the other flies out to give comfort to our fallen ideals. It is the inevitable change caused by the cosmic need to return to our path. The comfort in releasing our pre-conceived ideas is shown by the blessing of the golden yod. The female subconscious holds a red rose of love for future intent. The male, who is the conscious level, points to a new direction that he sees, even while he is still experiencing his fall. The top Tower windows already radiate the beginning of the new spiritual consciousness. As we look at the Tower we know there is always a new one to build. The key words are Cosmic Direction.

The Star is the male conscious level, now trying to comprehend the

THE STAR

THE MOON

universal consciousness. The tree of life is reaching out in new growth toward his head. A beautiful bird flies in the light of understanding, symbolizing the complete rebirth of spiritual freedom within the man. He is surrounded by his new inspiration. Around him are the gifts of new life. His hand has released the sword, and it is firmly lodged in the wall that leads to his new inner home. The tranquility of his garment reflects new established ideals and inspiration. The Star around his neck is one of perfect health and attainment on all levels. The staff of life is firm. He now looks to new and beautiful horizons of possibility. The lake of spirituality protects his new home, and the Star overhead will always remain in view. The key words are Health, Hope, and Aspirations.

The Moon card shows the man stepping forward from his crystal pool of contemplation. Using higher powers, he has allowed his subconscious to drink. His sword is cleansed and is reflected in the pool. The staff is nourished and the leaves are a richer green with fertile intent. He has manifested the pentacle, which is now engraved in stone. Behind him is his subconscious. She watches him walk away freely from doubt. As he approaches the two pillars he must retain his balance. He can see his new path at the dawn of new consciousness. With newfound earthly power and protected by the purple of the master's cloak, he steps forward to erase any further doubt. He looks up, sees the mystical Moon and allows his intuition to recognize the impregnation of the Sun, bringing together the known and the unknown. The golden yod fortifies and brings clarity. The key word is Intuition.

The Sun brings golden opportunity. Regardless of present circumstances, the Sun will bring personal joy. This golden sphere is surrounded by cherubs offering the gifts of life and opportunity. Each cherub brings a perfected tool to man. The sturdy cherub of Wands gazes directly into the sun of success. The cherub of Cups fills the chalice with golden opportunity and love. The Pentacle cherub points the way and the cherub of Swords is offering a rose of love. His sword is now sheathed in the red roses of love and no longer needs to be used. The four cherubs of the Sun surround the promise offered by this magnificent symbol. The blue spirituality of the sky upholds our needs and prayers. The Sun brings a message—the answer is yes. The key word is Attainment.

Judgement connotes self-judgment, rebirth, a renewal of the inner you. The higher consciousness is the child already emerging into the new existence. The child points the way, naked and void of all previous thought patterns. The female consciousness is dressed in a beautiful blue gown of spirituality. On her head and around her neck is a scarf of purity. She no longer wears shoes. She has recognized a new fertile world of life. The conscious level is the man in the process of reality. Before him is the book of life, his life. As he reads, his mind is filled with the light of new understanding. He has already removed his battle helmet. His right hand no longer needs the protection of the glove. As he now firmly holds the staff of life, his sword and shield are no longer required. He is in the process of self-judgment, self-analysis. It has been his greatest battle. The key word is Self-Analysis.

With the World card we are free to go in any direction, triumphant in any undertaking. The Fool has now concluded his journey. The wreath of flowers and leaves is given to the initiate when he has learned to use the four esoteric tools of life. The soul is rich with the experience of many lifetimes. The spiritual traveler has learned knowledge and understanding. He now has mastered the World and is aware of cosmic obligations. He is in command, and no longer depends on others. Clothed in the purple majesty of the master's veil, the victorious soul reaches easily to the universal powers, competent and unafraid. The key words are Victorious Completion. The soul is now ready to choose its path, the joy of true attainment remains and the merged levels of consciousness will be ever mindful of the effort and constant striving to reach this perfect point of existence.

GAIL FAIRFIELD

Creating, Maintaining and Enhancing Relationships

MY OWN BELIEF SYSTEM WITH REGARD TO relationships is that we have the notion of a relationship as though it were a "thing" —something we want to find, or create, or enhance. But in fact, relationships are not like houses or cars—they don't exist in the way that houses and cars exist. Relating is a process, and we are in the process of relating to ourselves and to all the significant others in our lives.

So it's useful to remember that a relationship is not something that we arrive at. In each of our lives we are always in the process of evolving our ability to relate. Even when we're not in a partnership with a significant other, we're still becomng more of who we want to be, so we can be in such a partnership, or happily single, or whatever we aim to be. Therefore, I think that relating is something we're often conscious of as human beings, no matter where we are in our own growth and evolution.

A lot of times when we think about relationships, or about relating, we think of love, or we think of a partner. But the other connections in our lives—family members, mentors, students, and so on—are also relationships that are at least significant. They just don't have the same romantic, story-telling quantity of literature written about them. They haven't become known in that way, but they are very, very important.

As we create relationships in our lives, there is a myth I think we have, especially the Western culture, that relationships happen by magic.

They come into our lives by magic, they leave our lives by magic or disaster, and we don't have much power or control over them at all. If they work, they work, and if they don't, they don't. Somehow we're never quite sure why. Then we see our therapist and figure out that someone reminded us of a parent, or my brother did that when I was seven, or I remember this, now I won't do that one again. And sure enough we don't do that again exactly, but we might do something *like* it again.

So, I think we spend a lot of our time in the magic and the mystique and the wonderment of how it's possible for relationships to work and function in our lives and how it's possible for them to make us so miserable. One of the things that is important to me is that we move those things that seem mystical into the realm of the real, that we try to de-mystify things. That's important to me in my work with the Tarot, and certainly important in my work with relating.

I believe that all the important relationships in our lives are actually created by us, whether we create them at the conscious or unconscious level. Somehow we send out little feelers and set it up so that we meet a person who is just like Daddy, or whoever. Other times we intentionally say, "Next time around, I don't care about commitment, I just want great sex." Or, "Next time around, all I want is somebody who's comfortable to watch TV with." We can sometimes set those things up consciously in our minds and actually go out and filter what's available in the community until we find that person. I think since we do this anyway at the unconscious level all the time, it behooves us to think about how to make whatever we're creating unconsciously become conscious.

To take that one step further, we might ask, "Why can't I have what I might not even know I want yet?" I think we've all come to that point where we say, "I deserve to have what I want." We've all heard that—it's a familiar refrain. If you know just what you want and you say affirmations and visualize, you can probably have what you want. But there are things we don't even know to want yet. "This is so far beyond my experience of what's possible, that I haven't evolved into wanting it yet." So those are two possible situations—when we know, we can imagine what we want in detail, and go out and find it—and when we don't know, we can add to our affirmation, "or better," "and something better." All of this applies when we consider the process of relating in connection with the Tarot.

To make relating a more conscious process, the first step I use is to identify the specific kinds of relationships I want—the specific kinds of people I want to have significance in my life. You can do this just with the cards if you want—put them down, pick out ten cards, and identify the characteristics of those cards. They might tell you ten different kinds of people you want. Or you can use more of a mental process. Here are some examples of kinds of people to relate to. There may be some you haven't thought of.

There's the level of the acquaintance. It's true that most of us don't actually seek acquaintances. Yet, acquaintances are often the people that oil our lives. As you go down the street, you see somebody you vaguely know, and you smile and they smile and you say "hello" and you go on. That's a little pleasant moment in the day. You might not stop and have tea together or lunch, but there's a sense that there's somebody out there who knows you and has acknowledged you. So acquaintances are one level of relating.

Then there are the myriad levels of friends. You can have just a basic-friend friend. You can have an intimate friend. Then you can have a sexual friend. You can have a friend who participates with you in a particular kind of endeavor or project; in other words, a spiritual-growth friend, or a let's-go-bowling friend. You can have friends that fit into certain directions you might be interested in. So, in the general category of friends there is a variety of types.

Then there are relationships with mentors, students, teachers, and all the people who help you grow and evolve—spiritual advisors, consultants, therapists. Do you want any of these people in your life right at the moment? Do you have them already? Have you thought to want any of them?

Then, of course, there's the broad-ranging group of relationships made up of family members. Sometimes people who don't have children of their own still want the experience of a child in their lives. I've had this in my life, when I've actually sought out another family to connect with when I didn't have kids in my life. I spent time with their kids because there was something about that kind of relationship that I really valued and treasured. Or, maybe your mother died when you were ten. You can undergo re-parenting and have a therapist be your "mother," but you can also just go find somebody down the street whom you can enjoy having as a mother figure. So family members, aside from the ones that we're biologically born to, can be people we choose as significant relationships in our lives.

Then there are the classic configurations of lover, partner, forever-and-ever mates, soulmates—whatever you want to call the intimates in your life. When you begin figuring out what you want to do about relationships in your life, and how you're going to make them better, I think the first step is to find out which kinds you actually want. Which ones have you had that you don't want anymore? What do you want to add in? Once you've done that, then you can look at your list and see how many types of relationships you want, and which of those you have are already working, so that you don't need to do anything about them. You might have listed ten different kinds of relationships you want, and find that you already have seven of them, and they're really fine. Of the three that are left, one of them's working well but needs some enhancement, one is really in the pits, and one is a kind you don't have. So those are the three you're going to work on. This process narrows the subject from all that might be possible to the real issues right now. There's a reason for doing this. Sometimes you discover, for example, that while moaning and groaning that you don't have a lover, all you really want is a go-to-the-movies-together-and-eat-popcorn friend. As you define those different categories, you see clearly what you truly want. And you might notice other things. Sometimes you're not looking in the right place for the person.

I knew a woman who was a recovering co-dependent, who had been in relationships with alcoholics her whole life, and it dawned on her one day that if she wanted to be in a relationship with non-alcoholics, she should stop going to bars to look for her next lover. It may seem obvious that if you're looking for something, you'd better look over here to find it instead of over there, but sometimes we don't see this unless we actually write it down: "This is truly what I'm looking to find; where's the appropriate place to find it?" Experiment. If you're looking for a child relationship, you don't have to find a lover who's childlike, you can go find a kid. There are lots of kids out there who need to be taken care of. So let's start with a relationship that doesn't exist, that you want to have in your life, in one of these kinds of categories.

The first thing that I like to use when I'm helping somebody figure out how to draw a relationship to them is a particular layout for creating a new relationship. The bottom line represents the status quo. I believe that if you don't have that particular kind of relationship in your life right now, there's some good reason why you don't. Maybe you're spending a lot of time at work, or you need time alone, or you're letting a past wound heal, or whatever it might be. There's some reason why it hasn't been appropriate up to now to have that particular form of relationship in your life. So the card at the bottom on the right asks, "What is the positive reason or the need for not having it now?" The bottom card on the left asks, "What is the positive reason or the need for creating it now?" Right above those two cards, you have the opportunity to discover what would be another

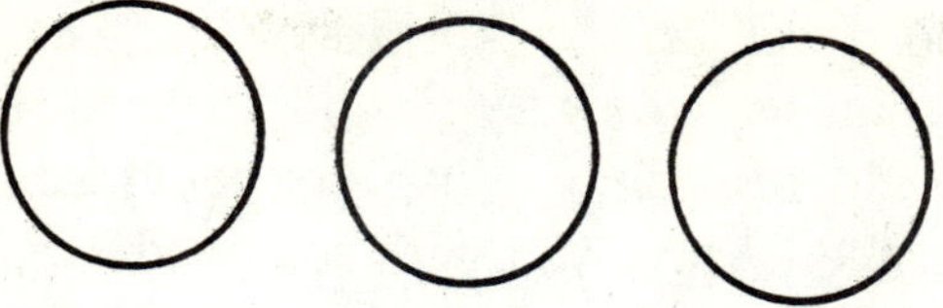

PROBABLE TIMING OF ARRIVAL OF THE "OTHER"—OPTIONAL TIMING ROW

RESHUFFLE

NEXT STEPS TO TAKE
(OPTIONAL—TIME FRAMES)

KEY QUALITIES TO
MAINTAIN/EXPRESS
IN THE SELF

KEY QUALITIES
TO SEEK IN THE OTHER

READING MAY END HERE

ANOTHER WAY
TO SATISFY THIS
REASON/NEED

ANOTHER WAY
TO SATISFY THIS
REASON/NEED

POSITIVE REASON/
NEED FOR
CREATING IT NOW

POSITIVE REASON/
NEED FOR NOT
HAVING IT NOW

CREATING A NEW RELATIONSHIP

© 1988 Gail Fairfield

way to meet that need. In other words, if there's a good reason for not having a relationship right now, how else could I take care of that reason and possibly still have a relationship? What else could I do about needing time alone? Maybe I could be involved with somebody who lives in a distant city. I'd have a lot of time alone but I'd still have that person. What might be another creative way to meet that need? And then on the left side, if there is a good reason to go ahead and proceed to discover or create that relationship, "What would be another way to take care of that need other than by this relationship?"

Then there's a line drawn, because sometimes after you lay out these four cards, the reading ends. The person looks at those questions and finds that there's a good reason for not having this kind of relationship right now. "I can't, because the only other way I could satisfy that need is something I don't want to do. So I'll take care of the relationship needs I have another way." These four cards are really a clarification of whether the relationship we claim we want is worth having. Sometimes we've assumed that that's what we wanted, but on reflection discover that it's not what we need.

Assuming then that it's still worthwhile to create a relationship, we go up to the next two lines. The first one is to learn what qualities to seek in the other person. There are just three cards there. Anyone who has been in the relationship process knows that we seek a lot more than three qualities in someone who's going to be significant in our lives. You can pull out fifteen cards or as many as you want; but if you start with at least three you'll see the core energy you want in that person, whether they're a mentor, a lover, or someone else.

The next row has to do with the key qualities in yourself that you want to be able to express in this relationship. In other words, what is it about you that's so important that you would not compromise it in that next connection? What is it about you that, when you love to ski and your partner doesn't, you'll even give up having them ski with you so long as that certain something about you can be preserved. It could be something you like to do. It could be your flamboyance. There is a certain part of me that likes to wear red and be "on stage." I've been in relationships where this would cause the other to say, "Calm down, ease up. Why are you doing this? Why don't you sit in the back row?" Needless to say, this did not do much for my self-image. So, what is it about yourself that you treasure enough to want to make sure it's enhanced and supported and valued and loved in your next relationship?

Then there's the row of, "What shall I do? What are the next steps to take?" I put two cards there and I wrote, "optional in time frame." You could put down six cards and consider them to be six months, asking what is the next step to take this month, next month, and so on. Or, you could just have them be the next general steps to take. You can also have the cards be sequential or simultaneous. You can create that line or that row of the layout any way you want. Note that whenever you're considering, say, the next step to take, if the cards are reversed, it frequently means that the step is an internal process. It's not an action you're going to take. It may be reflection, or an evaluation of your priorities. The upright cards are more inclined to be something you act on—put an ad in the paper, or whatever—an overt action. Here is another place where the reading may be concluded.

If you want to go on, I suggest you reshuffle, because the final row is for the probable timing of when this person you've now identified might come into your life. I have just three cards there, which could be three months, three years, or quarters of the year ahead, whatever you choose. You can identify that timing row anyway you want, but the reshuffling is very important because some of the cards that have already come up below might pop up in the timing row. I would say that eighty percent of the time I do this layout, something from the bottom comes up again.

There are two ways to do timing with the Tarot. One is that the card itself has the meaning. In other words, a three is three months, or three years, or three somethings. And the minor suits are associated with different seasons, so you can connect them with the third week of that season, for example. The other way, and the system that I prefer, is one in which you identify the time frame you want to think about. In other words, I may want to think about the year ahead, quarter by quarter, so I use the cards as first, second, third, and fourth quarters of the coming year. See what cards come up and which of them in its spirit most deals with the thing you're looking for. In other words, you might be saying, "When will the lawsuit be settled and when will I get the money?" If you get a nice Pentacles card, maybe the Eight of Pentacles, in the third quarter position, then you can pretty much say the money will probably come in the third quarter. Sometimes there's nothing, I can't find any money there. Then we either have to go farther ahead or move to a different tack, which might be, "What else do I need to be doing now to make this hapen?" That's a technique that works well for me. So you can designate any time frame you choose. I have some clients creating relationships they want in two months. Other people say, "Oh, just sometime within the next two or three years"—they're comfortable with a broad time frame. It's important to match your timing row with the personality and energy of the readee.

After you do the layout, you might want to make an affirmation tape to listen to. On it you could repeat, "I'm lovable, I'm loving, I deserve to have the kind of relationship I want," and so forth. Or you can make a collage, or write the sentences to be looked at over and over.

There are three levels to work on when you want a change to occur in your life, when you want to really pump it in. One is visual, seeing it in real pictures, seeing the words, or imagining it as a picture in your mind. The second is auditory, such as making tapes, or saying the sentences to yourself. The third level, which we do least often, is the feeling level: "How will I feel, what will I experience, when I have this?" You are trying on the depth of that experience and becoming familiar with it. "How will I feel if I have that wonderful mentor in my life, who truly cares about me and gives me superb feedback? Will that be a relief? Will that be exciting, or will it be threatening? What will my experience be inside?" The more you practice imagining an experience, the more inclined you are to attract to yourself the triggers and the catalyst that will bring you that feeling and experience. So when you're creating a future reality, whether it's a relationship or anything else, include the pictures, sounds and feelings of how that future might be for you.

The next stage is research. You have the model, the prototype, you've figured out what it is you want, and now it's time to go out into the world and meet people and interact with them. You keep this blueprint in the back of your mind, the kind of person you want and the kind of person you want to be. And you'll become more and more like that person you want to be as you make your search. You usually first attract someone who matches what you want, only to discover that you've left out some important details. And you find yourself interacting the way you thought you wanted to interact, only to discover that you've left out some other details. So, there's a little loop here, where you research and test and then come back and re-evaluate and add some more qualities, and then research and test again. You may go through several abortive connections with people before you arrive at the blueprint that's going to work for you.

I've known people who end up with lists of fity or eighty qualities in themselves or the other person that they feel need to be there for the relationship to work. You can't do this with Tarot cards. So, it becomes fascinating and very specific. You see that everything that occurs and every connection you make is part of the experiment. It's important to think, not about failure, but about what this tells you. What is this feedback about? This also keeps you from just waiting—that state of "someday it will come, I'm waiting." Six months go by and you're still waiting. That is not a pleasant place to be. Instead, research and re-evaluate your criteria, and change them; then research some more, so that you're always in the process. Even if it takes you five years to find that surrogate mother you're looking for, or the lover you've desired, you've been creating the relationship all that time, and you've also been evolving and becoming more of who you need to be to have it materialize. So I think that loop is significant. And each time in the loop, after you research and re-evaluate, you can do another Tarot reading, and chart your next course.

With these kinds of Tarot readings I enjoy keeping a record of them, maybe in a file folder. If you do them every day—or week, or month—however fast you want to go—and watch them as they evolve, you can look back and remember where you were. "Why, at the beginning I thought the most important thing was somebody who kept their word and was punctual, and now everybody I meet is punctual. So that's not the most important thing anymore. Now I realize I've moved on to someplace else." You can watch yourself evolve if you keep track of your readings about a specific subject. That's the process I use to attract a new kind of person into my life or in readings for others.

Now, let's assume that the other case is true, and that you have a particular relationship, but it isn't going as well as you'd like. You can use a layout for dealing with an existing relationship. At the bottom it asks, "What's the reason why the relationship exists this way right now? What's the positive reason for it?" Does the fact that the relationship is the way it is keep you from being scared? Does it satisfy the needs of your family? Does it provide a lot of security that allows you to go out and grow and do other things that are important in your life? What's the point of having this relationship in your life right now, as it exists? And the card right next to it says, "What would be the point of changing it?"

You can have three cards in each of those positions. You don't have to have just one reason to keep the relationship the way it is, or one reason to change it—you can have more than one. But that's the first place to begin. In the next row up, the cards answer the question, "What would be the way or ways to satisfy your needs?" So, if you're staying in this relationship because it provides financial security, you may discover that there's another way of handling this need so that you have a choice again.

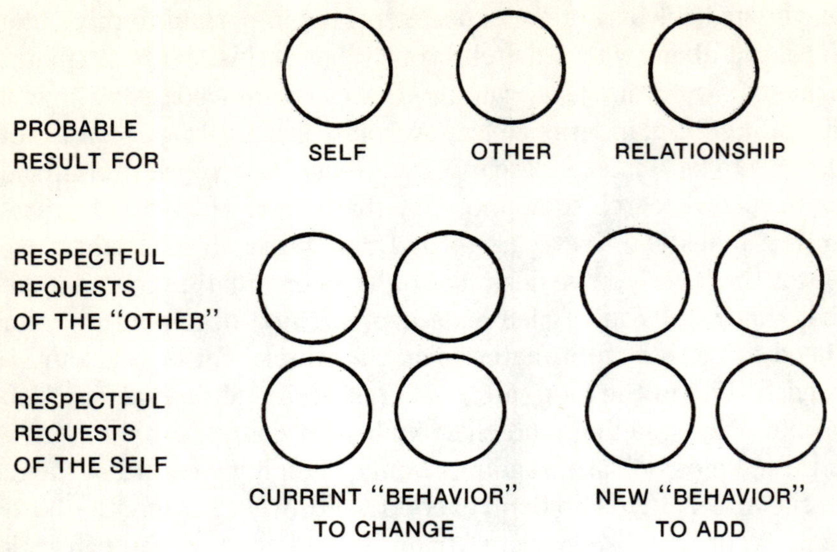

READING MAY END HERE

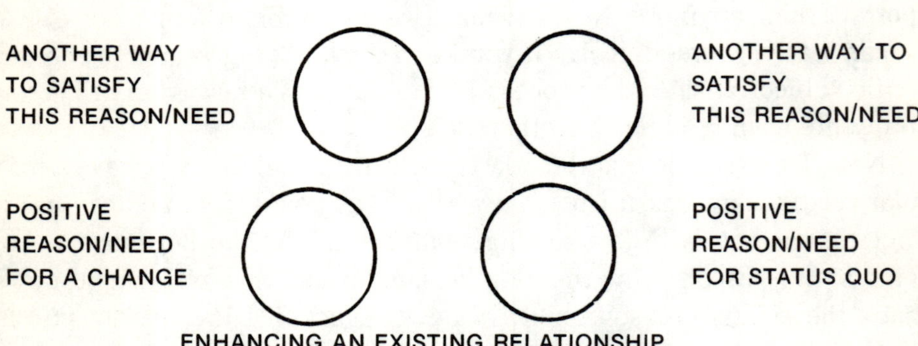

Choice is an important word for me, and it's important to remember that creating a relationship or having a relationship evolve is always a choice. This person is not with me simply because they've been with me for ten years. This person is with me because we are in a process of relating. I still choose them every morning, and they still choose me every morning. Or at least once a week. Sometimes when you wake up in the morning, you're not going to say, "I want to be with my partner." By choosing them every day, I don't mean that you wake up every day and re-evaluate whether you should break up. I mean there's a reason why you're still drawn together. It's not a thing, you didn't acquire it like a thing, it's a continuous process. Again, the reading can end after these first four cards if you discover that you don't want to change the relationship, that the cost would be too great, it wouldn't be worth it.

I know that if you've done readings for yourself or for others you've had the experience of people saying, "No, no, no," and "I wish she would change," and "I wish she would do that, and why can't this be better," and so on. But when you really think about it, sometimes we're not willing to do whatever it would take to make the changes because it's not worth the cost. I think that's okay. The important thing is that it's conscious, that a decision is made, and you say, "This is my choice—it's not by default. I'm not just slipping into it, it's my conscious choice."

If the reading doesn't end here and you decide you want to enhance this relationship, then there are two ways in which the relationship can grow. One is to change current behavior—everything from what you say to yourself to how you feel, to what you do. Behavior isn't just someone never giving you roses on your birthday—it's all the ways of being in the world. So, you can change current behavior to enhance a relationship. And the other thing that can be done is simply to add new behavior. You're not changing anything that exists, you just get to have more. I do a lot of readings for couples, and one concept that seems to really delight them is that you can learn to do someone else's style of something without giving up your own. In other words, you can learn to enjoy a certain kind of movie. Or, a person who likes to get up and accomplish tasks on Saturday might be in a relationship with a person who likes to stay in bed all day until at least one or two, then maybe laze through the newspaper and a cup of coffee, and by about five or six in the evening is ready to do something. This has come to symbolize everything about their whole relationship and everything that they are: "You never want to," and "You always want to." It always comes as a surprise that you can add the other person's behavior patter to your life without losing yours. It might enhance you to experiment with that—it doesn't have to be an either/or situation. There doesn't have to be a right way to be, a "better" way to be. For example: "Hey, man, I'm really cool and laid back and I take it easy all day," versus, "I'm very responsible and organized and I get things done." Which is right? They're both right. Taking turns doing it the other person's way and then your way might enhance your life, might add without subtracting. Learning how another person is in the world, modeling them, copying them, if you will, trying it their way, doesn't have to be a denial of your way. It can be a nice addition. The new behavior might even be something you like that you didn't know to want.

When you do want another's behavior to change, I recommend a respectful request. You really can't change anybody—you really can't say, "You *have* to do this." What you can say is, "I respectfully request this. Will you consider it? On nights when I have to get up at five the next morning, will you watch TV in the other room so I can go to sleep?" That's a request. And it's a respectful request. The person has the choice to say no, and then you may leave. In any case, there is a category of respectful request for a behavior change. And if there is one that you think is needed, it will come out in this row in the layout. If your respectful request is done in a mode of being in this together, not you versus me, my needs versus yours, but *our* needs, then sometimes your requests will be responded to. Sometimes they won't, and then you have to be able to detach yourself. If the person says no, you have to accept that. Then you have to do another little mini-layout of how else to get your needs met. Ask, "What else can I do now?"

Probably the more important row here is the respectful request of the *self*. What are the things you will caringly, lovingly respectfully ask *yourself* to change or add to your behavior? And again, in this row you can have five things, three things, as many as you want, that you want to either add or change about who you are.

Sometimes you might get a strange card, and it's important to keep in mind the position it's in. For example, you might want to change a behavior and you get, say, the Queen of Cups. Among other things the Queen of Cups has a lot to do with emotional maturity and good relationship skills. If that card is in the position of a current behavior to change, it might be a little confusing at first, until you look at the negative side, the possible negative implications of say, knowing it all and always being perfect. How is it that you communicate so clearly and handle relationships so well that you can't ever be wrong? So sometimes the card that in another context would show desirable characteristics indicates the very thing that might be in the way of your being able to interact intimately with somebody else. After all, intimacy implies vulnerability, a willingness to bare the soul a little bit. Even though you may be very mature about relationships, you might need to remember that this is a new person, or that this is a specific relationship, not a generic one, and that you're not "doing" a relationship, you're relating to a person with flesh and blood and feelings. So sometimes you have to remember the position the card is in and interpret it accordingly.

For example, the temptation with the Queen might have been to say, "Oh, you don't have to change anything, you're already good at relationships—there's nothing to change." The top row in this layout is the probable result for yourself, for the other person, and for the relationship as a whole. If these changes do occur, what will happen? Sometimes it's going to be better; sometimes you'll know that you've done everything you can and that it's probably going to fall apart; but at least you'll know that you've done what you could.

I say probable results because moving into the future is always a probability. At this given moment in time, right here, right now, there are a million different futures that could occur. And, given who I am and the choices I've made in the past, there are far fewer futures than a million that are truly probable. But even those are quite a few different futures. As a result of the reading, you might think about that and make a different choice, take an action, change something. Then the probabilities switch around again.

So, when you're in a serious re-evaluation process with regard to relationships, I think it's important to be aware of what's going on by doing frequent readings. If you're paying someone for the readings, you probably wouldn't go every week—you'd probably go once a year or every six months. If you're doing readings for yourself, you can do them frequently enough to stay current with your situation and not base what you do today on where you might have been six months ago, though it's also interesting to see that evolution.

After you've done your layout, it's useful to practice presenting your request. There are a number of ways to do this. You can look in the mirror

and decide what kind of expression you want to have. Is this a demand—
"I want you to do this"—or is it a request—"Do you think maybe somehow, sometime five years from now, you could . . . ?" Neither of those is
very likely to give you the results you want. There are other ways in between those two extremes. Choose the persona, the part of you that can
best present your particular request to the other person.

And choose the timing. Sometimes I amaze myself when I work on
an intimate relationship between eleven at night and one in the morning,
even though I have to be up at seven. It's foolishness! We would be better
off sleeping than dealing with our relationship at that time of night. Timing is very important. When somebody is getting ready to go to work, or
when the kids are screaming, it's not the correct time to present your
respectful request. So think about your approach—how you're going to
look, what your tone should be, what you're going to ask for, and when.

After you practice, go out and try it. If you don't get what you want,
go back and try something else. After you've done that five or six times
and you still don't get what you want, then you have to re-evaluate things.
Is it worth it? There are always those points at which you ask, "Is it worth
it?" In enhancing your relationship it's vital to remember that this process
is an experiment—you screwed up your courage and asked the person,
and they didn't even know what you were talking about. They said things
like, "I do what? Everybody does that." Or, "I don't even know what you
mean." This is really a depressing moment. But if you can remember that
this was an experiment—something about the language you chose, or
something you were doing didn't make it clear what you were after—then
you can change that and go back.

There are, of course, serious cases in which the person is drunk and
denying it, or maybe truly doesn't know. Then nothing is going to make a
difference—they're not going to get it. So you have to decide whether it's
worth pursuing your respectful request and presenting what you're working on. This is the experimental phase. You try something, then you come
back and look at more cards to see what you should try next. Then you try
that, and continue this process until everything says drop it, it's done, or
we've arrived there now. It's an ongoing process.

If you do decide that this relationship you wanted to enhance isn't going to have a future, there is another layout you can use to gracefully conclude or transform a relationship. Ending or changing relationships can be
traumatic. Maybe they're always traumatic for you, but they can be gracefully traumatic or just nasty. You can't always be graceful, but it's worth

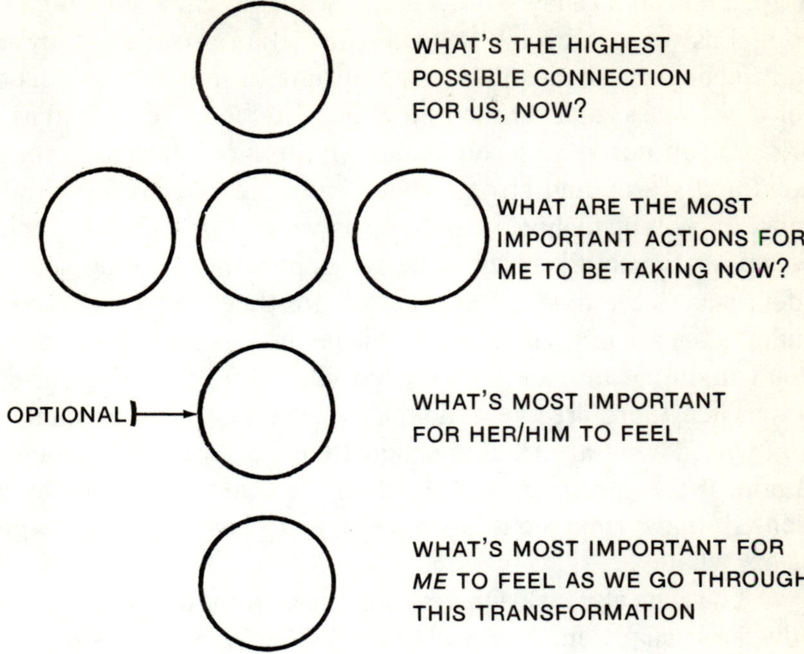

GRACEFULLY CONCLUDING OR TRANSFORMING A RELATIONSHIP

a try. You can do a layout that starts with, "What's most important for me to feel as we go through this transformation process? Is my most important feeling that it wasn't a waste of time for me to be in this relationship for eight years? Is it for me to feel that I'm being respected as an equal as we split up our record collection? My opinion matters here. Is it to feel solid and sturdy and strong, that I can take care of myself? What is the most important feeling I can have as we end or transform this thing that was a relationship?" If you want to support the other person, you can ask them what's the most important way for them to feel. Or you can just let them take care of themselves at this point. You may have done as much as you can do. Dealing only with what you want to feel is your choice.

Then there are the action steps; you can have as many of them as you want. What are the important things for you to be doing right now? Again, if the card is reversed, these are internal doings—to say affirmations, to have time alone, to remember to love yourself, to get plenty of sleep, whatever.

You can also ask what the highest potential for this connection is now, and usually one card will tell you. The highest possible thing is not to have this person in your life anymore, ever. Or, the highest possible thing may be that all along the relationship was a mental connection and you were trying to make it a love relationship, so now you can move it over to where it truly belongs in your life.

With a little layout like this, you can discover where to expect the relationship to go, what to hope for, what to intend, and what you need to hold on to for yourself. What's the core? What's the driving force? What's the centering emotion you need to hold on to as you go through this transition? All these questions can help you learn how to change a relationship gracefully.

MARY K. GREER

Healing Emotional Pain
with the Tarot

PEOPLE ALWAYS SAY THERE'S NOTHING NEW under the sun, and I've found that to be very, very true with Tarot. Tarot is a book of ageless wisdom, of knowledge of the path we travel to know ourselves. So Tarot should contain pretty much everything, in one form or another. We may not be able to find it in the cards at a particular time, but that doesn't mean the potential isn't there.

I find that when I invent something new—a new spread or a new way of perceiving the cards—within a couple of weeks or months somebody comes along with exactly the same thing. The first time it happened I had invented a spread in which you draw one card from all the court cards, one from the Minor Arcana number cards, and one from the Major Arcana, so that you have a little three-card spread. And then I read *Magical Ritual Methods*, by William Butler, and lo and behold! the spread was in there, so I hadn't invented it after all! It was there, waiting for people to come across it. This happens to me over and over: I'll see something new and the next week I'll bump into somebody who says, "Oh, I just found this wonderful new thing in the Tarot," and it will be the same thing.

When the time is right, a lot of people see the same thing simultaneously. It was exciting for me to receive dozens of letters about my three books from people saying, "You wrote the book I wanted to write." In fact, I just happened to be the person who got a particular attitude out there first. It wasn't that it hadn't been going on, or that people weren't teaching the same things.

I find that other people's work with Tarot often stimulates my own work. I had been teaching Tarot in Florida for several years as an unaccredited college course. Then I moved to San Francisco, where I taught it for about ten years as an accredited course in an undergraduate school, New College of California. Then a friend of mine told me about a fantastic teacher who was using Crowley's Thoth deck, also called the Crowley-Harris deck, after its wonderful artist, Frieda Harris. The teacher was Angeles Arrien, and it was from her classes that I learned to open myself up and break all the rules. I had already been doing that sort of surreptitiously, but I learned from Arrien that it was okay. She actually threw out Crowley's writings because they just didn't speak to her. She looked at the pictures and images and said, "These are cross-cultural symbols, they will speak to anyone. You don't need a book to find out what they really mean. That something transcended even that original vision."

That doesn't mean you have to throw out Crowley, not by any means; that was just her approach. The point is that from her I realized that I can throw out anything when something else speaks to me. And so I do, regularly. Often I'll throw something out just to see what happens, what comes up then.

I also use the cards, especially the Major Arcana and the elemental suits— the idea of fire, air, earth, and water—as my pigeonholing system whenever I read anything. You can pick up almost any book in my library and find the High Priestess or the Hierophant written all up and down in the margins—in anthropology, archeology, psychology, and the science-fiction fantasy novels that I love.

After a while I start to see ideas come together. So I recommend to those of you who think in terms of the cards to use that as your basic note-taking system.

When I was reading *The Nature of Personal Reality*, a Seth book by Jane Roberts, I discovered that the ideas I was pigeonholing were coming up in the sequence of the Major Arcana cards. This really surprised me, and it later became one of the basic ideas for my book *Tarot Mirrors*. They corresponded all the way through the Seth book. At one point I thought they weren't going to correspond, because where the Death card should be, the subject was about a creative burst of life energy. I thought, "No, wait a minute, Death is supposed to be here, Seth. You've been going along all the way to Thirteen; you're not going to fail me now, are you?"

Two pages later Seth says, "By the way, what I mean by this creative life energy is what is known on your planet as death," and I said, "Thank you, Seth." It was almost as if it were a direct response to my question, and a confirmation.

There is a pattern of network to our experiences, a form. We are in the world of form. Anybody who has a sense of that form will describe it in whatever terminology or vocabulary they are used to using. The Tarot was created by someone who saw the structure, the form of that reality. It's there in the Tree of Life. It's there in *The Nature of Personal Reality.*

Another person who sees these patterns and came out with a similar system is Bill Lammey. In his *Karmic Tarot* Lammey sees a pattern that actual expands for me what I've seen. It gives me a whole new perspective. His system relates to work being done now with addictions and in twelve-step programs, and so on, understanding the underlying patterns behind all that. And that's what healing emotional pain is all about—getting a sense of the pattern that is there underneath our pain. Once we have a sense that there is this web, this pattern, we can make our way along it, and work our way through it. We can see that all experiences might be there for a purpose, that it's part of an overall tapestry. It's not just some little dangling thread, with us clinging to the end of it, about to fall off into the abyss at any moment. We are actually part of this tapestry, a whole picture. Looking at the Tarot from this perspective can help us work through things when we're in the depths.

Another point about the experience of discovering something new, in whatever perspective, is that it starts coming up in your life everywhere. I'm sure you've noticed that. You see something new and then it seems to appear everywhere. When I started working on this lecture and studying the idea of healing emotional pain, right in the middle of it my life fell apart in emotional pain. I was in agony—I went running to a therapist and said, "Help, I need to get some perspective on all this." And in telling her who I was, I handed her a copy of my book *Tarot Mirrors*, which contains a piece on emotional healing, and a process for it. The next week I went back and she said, "Healing emotional pain, huh? Have you been using the process in your book?" I said, "No, I'm in too much pain."

That's another thing: We learn a lot of wonderful processes, but sometimes we just don't want to use them. We want to stay in our pain. We want to stay in our problem. That's all right. Don't beat yourself up over doing that. You might even be starting to pull yourself out of a problem, only to put yourself right back in by saying, "I didn't use all those things I could have used." I feel it's sometimes appropriate to just be wherever you are, that you don't have to immediately fix things. There's a time for going into the underworld journey, and you can't learn if you cut it off too quickly. We shouldn't put ourselves down, we should acknowledge and thank ourselves for giving ourselves whatever we needed. So, in healing emotional pain, don't try and heal it too quickly, before you're ready. Sometimes just be with it, no matter how painful it is. That's part of the process.

When the therapist pointed this out to me I realized it was now time for me to start using my own techniques. And I found that they do help! I got a lot of reinforcement from that.

The cards are a mode of divination. I define divination as "discovering the will of spirit." Divination comes from the word "divine" or "deva." Deva is a term for god or goddess. So, by using all the tools of divination, you can open communication with Spirit. The primary reason for doing this is to discover those things we can't sense through our normal means of seeing, discussing, or observing. Something may be hidden from our view because we can't possibly know it yet, it's in the future; or it's a subconscious process we can't see; or it's something in the past we repressed and therefore we don't consciously know. Divination also works for things we know we don't know, as when something is lost or stolen. Some people are very successful at this.

In thinking specifically about emotional pain, there's a little process you can use to begin the work. With it, you can discover some area in which your emotions are very sensitive. Perhaps the emotions are hidden, or if not quite hidden, right now you're just not as fully aware of the emotions in a given situation in your life as you could be.

You can do this with a partner or by yourself. Take your deck and quickly shuffle the cards, or just spread or fan them face down in front of you, and choose a card. We are looking for a hidden emotion, something it's appropriate for you to look at right now. Then simply describe the card, as if to a person who can't see it. Just use a couple of sentences. When you've described your card, what it looks like, stop and repeat what you just said but use the "I am" form. Be sure you repeat what you actually said. Then pause for a second and think of how that most applies to your life at present. What issue does it bring up that you have been dealing with? Just think for a second to yourself, and connect with where in your life you've been experiencing that.

Now you have some emotional situation, a place where your emotions are invested, that's important for you to look at. There might be some insight, some new thought that comes up, some connection that will be made around that emotional issue, and what's going on with it. As soon as you bring something into consciousness you start finding signs of its significance everywhere. I sometimes use that process for myself when I find I'm just looking at a card and thinking I know what it means, but in fact I haven't really said to myself what it means. Then I take myself through that process. Also, after all these years, I still find I can turn up a card in a reading and look at it in panic, thinking I don't know what it means. So as a basic rule, when in doubt, describe the card. Then you can turn that description into questions to draw out the readee and their experience, or to ask yourself. Out of that description will often emerge the card's significance at that moment. Every time you describe a card, no matter how well you know it, you will describe it differently. You will discover things that you had never seen before, or never noticed, or hadn't thought about in years.

There are more ways of developing that exercise enumerated in my book *Tarot Constellations*, and there is a review in *Tarot Mirrors*. You can extend the process by looking a little more deeply at the attitudes and mood of the card and by making up stories, fairy tales, or "what if" stories about the card. Just based on the card itself, you can discover the information that is important for that moment, without having to go to any books, or even to your own rote memory of what the card is supposed to mean. You can let each card be its own unique self and speak to you in that moment, by using this technique. The deck you use will color the interpretation with its own image, feeling, and emotion portrayed on the card.

Emotions come from an old, old concept which has been revised often and discussed in many ways, but I like going back to what the ancient Greeks said. Before they came up with the four elements, they were playing around with the question of the most basic element out of which the whole earth had evolved. One of them came up with the idea of it being a Venus-Mars conflict. Those were the basic elements, in other words—attraction and repulsion—and everything on this planet came out of the interplay of those two energies. Magnetism—attraction and repulsion—were thought to be the most basic elements before earth, air, fire, and water were seen as elements. These were seen as abstract elements, but they are really the basic elements of emotion.

In Paul Foster Case's book *The Tarot* and in other philosophical works, I kept reading that life is a road of desire. I'd say, That's nice, that's one I can memorize and repeat in my classes, but I never understood what it meant until I started trying to deal with this emotional pain issue. Then I realized that life is like the Chariot with those two sphinxes:

we are pushed and pulled by our feelings toward what we are attracted to and away from what we are repulsed by. And that's how we make our way down our life path. That's how we learn.

We learn through what we are attracted to and what we are repulsed by. What we are attracted to, we call desire. I desire this, I want this, I'd really like to have that. You know that turquoise top over in the dress shop? Yes, I desire that. But I am also repulsed by the amount of money it costs. So on the other hand is fear, anxiety—oh no, it costs too much. I can't do that to my poor family. My daughter won't be able to eat. All these unreasonable fears come up if I think of giving in to desire, and push me away from the thing I desire. So the other side of desire is fear, and the tension between them is experienced as conflict and anxiety.

Rather than seeing these things as mechanisms we don't have any control over, or as Fate, we can see them as teachers. These are the things that have been given to us to teach us how to get through life. Life is a string of desires. You can trace through your life how those desires change and how your fears change. Something that you were fearful of at one point in your life—like getting up in front of a group of people and speaking— you may be on the path of dealing with now. After a while it's not the fearful thing it was at first. It may even become desirable. Our desires also become more and more defined. Most of us can look back and see how something that once had control over us we've now refined, and perhaps found a new desire. It's not that we don't desire the other thing as much as it is that we've found a desire that's more important, and we're willing to sacrifice the old to have the new one.

So, whenever there is pain, that is part of this great life teacher, this dichotomy, which is often called "the Teacher Who Bites," and we learn from that. The thing to do first is say thank you, because by expressing gratitude, you become aware and begin transforming the painful emotions —the fear, the anxiety, the conflicts—into something you can learn from and eventually begin equating with desire. Thus, all opposites merge into a new entity.

If we look at the 22 Major Arcana from The Rider-Smith-Waite deck and have the Fool represent us going through the Major Arcana, we can see how they each relate to the concept of emotions, the string of desires, and how we learn from them.

The Magician card shows you at the beginning of the path. When you're looking through the cards like this, one of the important things to notice is where red appears, because if you remember your symbology,

red equals burning desire, lust. So here you have yourself as the Magician cloaked in your desire and focusing all your intention on cultivating the garden of your desires— the roses and lilies on the card. The roses are the red roses of your physical desires, and the lilies are the desire for truth, which is also the path along which desire can lead you.

Continuing on this journey with the Magician as number one, in number two you have the realization of the other. The Magician, as you can imagine, is the baby, who is only aware of the I: I want, I'm hungry. The first fear of the child is of falling—it's an automatic reflex. Also there is the urge to suck, so there you have the basic desire and fear. By the time you know what it is you're sucking, you have the sense of the self that's over here, but you need this other thing that's over there. When you don't get what you want, you begin setting up the duality of the self and the other, which is separate. Later on in life it becomes the good and the bad, or what I want and what I don't want, what I am and what I'm not. This is what the two pillars, black and white, of the High Priestess card represent. I am the good mother, and of course I'm none of those things that a bad mother is, so that's somebody else over there. There are the good guys and the bad guys, the Republicans and the Democrats, all those different dualities. You're usually certain that if you work at it you will find the right one and the wrong one. And they are all attached to your memories either from this lifetime or previous lifetimes, when these desires were fulfilled and felt good, or weren't fulfilled and you were punished. Your

THE HIGH PRIESTESS

THE EMPRESS.

Magician conscious mind wants one thing on the surface, and your High Priestess subconscious mind wants something else underneath, that you may or may not be aware of—that hidden thing you can use the Tarot to discover.

So you turn to the High Priestess, your intuition, your oracle, to find out about the inner dichotomies, and from their interplay comes the birth of a possibility of integration, a new way of seeing things. That is the pregnant Empress, who in a sense creates the reality you experience. The Empress also reminds you that you like to have your comfort. You want to rest in what feels good to you, be clothed in the sensual things you desire. She has made her garden of desires grow.

Sometimes, though, you have to be careful of these desires because they can grow like weeds—want, want, want, have to have—the whole matter of luxuries that Venus is sometimes accused of, just wanting more and more growth. Then the Emperor comes along in your life and says there has to be a limit to growth. You have to put some boundaries on it. You will define the township like this, this is your area, and this is my area. Then you come to punishment and rules—you can have this but you can't have that. Often that occurs through the interplay of the archetypal mother, who gives to you and nurtures you, and the archetypal father who sets the limits and tells you the world doesn't like this or that, you have to be more socially conscious. These are the rules: You don't cross the street without looking. The red mountains in the background of the Emperor

signify the heights of your aspirations, which the Emperor is pointing out to you. He is the father who says, You can grow up to be a doctor; being a potter is not going to make you any money. He wants to show which are the proper sorts of desires, and which aren't. So there are sometimes a lot of issues to deal with when this card comes up. Are the rules appropriate any longer or not? Which ones are you still living under, and which ones do you want or not want?

Similarly, with the Hierophant you have the religious constructs that tell you what's right and what's wrong, what's spiritual and what's not. When you go to school, when you work for a corporation, you are trained in what you're supposed to desire in your work and what you're not. These dichotomies are always there. With the Hierophant you have somebody who says, I have the answer. If you follow my rules you won't have any more conflicts. Just stick with the dogma, with this way of doing things. That's the gray pillar. There might be a way of resolving this; if you can find the right teachers they will show you the road. Part of your learning is ultimately to find your inner teacher—what used to be called the conscience.

As you continue to grow you come to the Lovers card. One of your greatest teachers in the area of emotion is relationships. Emotions are played out through your relationships. In adolescence you reach that point where your desire to be considered good by your parents is in direct conflict with your desire to feel good with a partner. And so you have the

Lovers' issues to deal with. In the writings of many of the mystics, the image of sexual relationships, the idea of physical unity, is the model for what is later seen spiritually as a higher desire for finding that unity with Spirit.

Next is the Chariot. In the familiar pattern of laying the cards in three rows of seven, the seventh card, the Chariot, ends the first row. Here is someone who has gained control of our physical desires. I can handle chocolate. Just say no. Here you have the master, the victor who has learned how to handle these things, who is in charge. A lot of people think personal development stops here—I can control the feelings I have. And, so you go through life thinking you are in charge of everything.

If you desire to go on, and often even if you don't, you come across Strength. In the Rider deck, the next card is Stength. Life's path continues. Whether you choose to continue on or not, you still come to Strength, the beginning of the second row of cards. One of the things you discover with the Strength card is that with the red, desire, your real strength comes from befriending your desires, from being in touch with them, not by repressing them or trying to keep a tight leash on them. This is the red lion. By learning to balance those energies you gain inner strength—the fortitude to get through what are often very difficult times in life.

Anger is one of the big clues that hidden emotions have been touched on, and anger comes up a lot in the Strength card. It can also be lust. For myself, I tend to get really angry, angry beyond all proportion, at certain

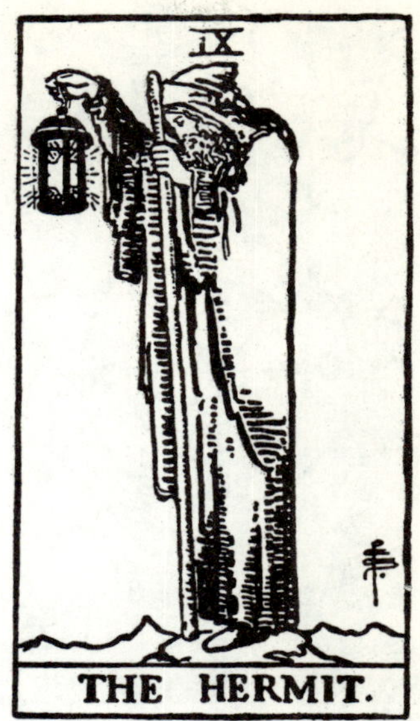

things. People want you to "get hold of your anger," but I've learned that I need to find out what the lesson is in that anger. I need to acknowledge it, to befriend it like the maiden befriending the lion. Usually anger covers up a deeper emotion. It might be a fear of abandonment, it might be fear of being unloved, an inability to communicate, a fear of loss. It could be about two beliefs that suddenly I find are in conflict. Here I thought this power was white and that one was black and now I find they're not, and rather than deal with that, I get angry at so-and-so who brought it up. You need to be able to see this and learn from it. Anger is very important and you need to thank your anger, look at the deeper feelings behind it.

With the Hermit, you've been climbing a long road learning about your desires, learning what you fear. You come to a certain point where you stop and observe where you've come from. You look back at all those experiences and relationships and say, What did they teach me? You might see a role model, someone who talks about their life, and suddenly you can see that their life wasn't always easy. They went through a lot. For the first time you get a sense of the light of truth—that's the lantern, a sense that your desire might be leading you to what is sometimes called "purity."

A sense of wholeness, a possible unity, the integration of the elements, are found in the Star, and you begin to feel that this might be possible for you. So you dedicate yourself to following your desires. You realize that if you work at them and learn from them, they can lead you somewhere. Ah, what an idea, that our desires can be our teachers.

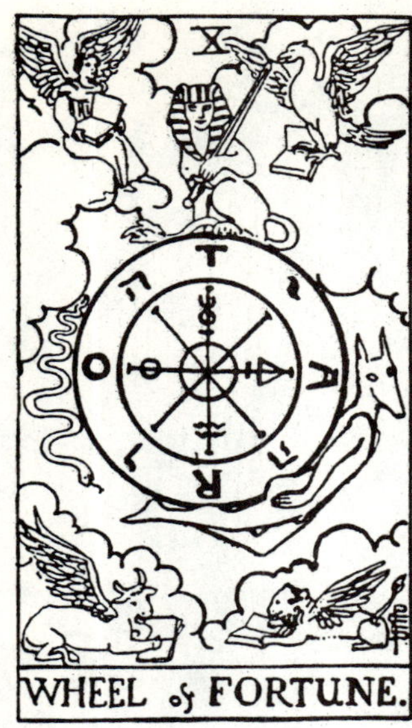

Of course, it seems that whenever you have these insights something comes along to throw you for a loop. You're given the big lesson, the big test, to see how well you've learned. You thought you were up on top of the mountain and all of a sudden you find you're down in the abyss.

The Wheel of Fortune allows you to experience change. It allows you to discover that it's possible to see in a new light things that had previously been fearsome or caused anxiety. So in Justice we discover there are certain desires, certain patterns, that you can judge with the sword and perhaps end the cycle, to get out of any ruts you've been in.

With the Justice card, you evaluate and judge the worth of your feelings. Sometimes anger is justified. Its expression may have been excessive for the reality of the situation—that's something you have to learn how to deal with—but you shouldn't put down the feeling, because it's based on something real. With Justice you strive to discover the truth in your own life. You can become your own fair witness, acknowledge your anger, and then evaluate the situation to find the truth. There is always a grain of truth somewhere, no matter how outrageous or unreasonable the situation may seem. You're being told about a deeply hidden conflict, anxiety, or fear you have. Once you can begin bringing this up, and become conscious and aware of it, you can decide how you want to handle it, what you want to do. And so in the Hanged Man you look at whatever patterns you have been stuck in, in order to be able to see them in a completely new perspective, a new light. You don't need to be "hung up" anymore.

In dealing with emotional pain, in going through a healing process to bring back some kind of harmony, you face issues that make you feel out of ease, dis-eased. To get at the depths of those issues, a sacrifice is necessary. One of the major sacrifices you have to make is voluntarily choosing to let go of whatever it is in the past you're holding onto. Like the Hanged Man, we have to look at things from a new point of view. Some of us identify ourselves by the ways we've been hurt. Are you willing to let go of that? To let go of what your mother or your father did to you, what the school system did to you? It's a great sacrifice to let go of your reason for not succeeding, but you have to if you're going to go on. Once you make that choice and let go, you can sever those things that are no longer necessary. And that's the Death card. Sometimes anger in a current relationship is actually about a previous relationship. So you have to let go of your anger at your current partner, or your current situation, because you actually have to deal with the old one. You must sever all the dead branches to see what the real issue is. You need to get down to what's still alive, where the growth is really possible, and then a new spurt of growth can emerge.

You leave one room, the room of your past angers, or where you have been placing them recently, which may not be where you were really angry, and you enter a new room. You make a transition. Doing that brings reconciliation, which is what Temperance is about. You can look at your partner and say, I'm not angry at you, it was just my fear of nobody listening to me. I felt that you weren't listening to me like everybody else

wasn't listening to me, like my mother didn't listen to me. This allows reconciliations and an ability to rebalance and find a way to communicate so that the old anger doesn't return. You find ways to bring a healing. Find some perspective through which to integrate your emotions. You have to put your feet on the ground and be practical; like Temperance you have to soar to the heights of your fiery inspirations and bring in the airy quality of clear thinking in order to blend all of them. Temperance represents the healing that comes after cutting off what's not really necessary to your emotional actions in your contemporary life.

After that it's time to look at your shadow, those things that you think you aren't. There's a bright shadow and a dark shadow. The bright shadow would say, Oh, I wish I could be an artist and create a beautiful new Tarot deck, but I'm just not artistic. The bright shadow is something in you that's artistic, some way in which you could create that deck, if you chose to. It's your choice.

This is fifteen, the Devil. One and five add up to six, like The Lovers, which is often called the choice card. The Devil is another card of choice. It's your choice whether you choose to own your shadow. The dark shadow is like an administration that ruins the environment and the economy. It's all the things you fear in yourself, about how you're ruining your own economy. Are you taking in people's words without really hearing them? How many people do you send off to war because of your anger? You're not always sensitive. So, owning your shadow is finding who the scapegoats are

and looking at them. When you do that, you achieve tremendous knowledge about yourself. The Devil card represents all the things that keep you from knowing yourself. It's also called the Pan card, which means being completely who you are without any restrictions, without any of the "shoulds" and "oughts" that are placed on you by the Emperor and the Hierophant. Remember back when you were told, Don't do this and don't do that, and forever after you felt guilty about it. "The devil made me do it." When you begin owning up to those things you release tremendous knowledge about yourself. When that happens, a bolt of insight hits you and you break out of the Tower of your limitations, out of all the structures that hold you back, so that the clear light of insight breaks through. That's the ideal.

Unfortunately, you'll go through times when you're not quite ready to acknowledge your shadow side. Then life gives you a bolt out the blue that can shatter you. You know you should leave your job. You've been meaning to for six months. The next day you get fired. This happens when we avoid facing our fears. The Tower, acting as fate, breaks through everything that's been holding you back. So it's time to deal with this particular fear.

You can also use the Tower to shatter those things that have been closing you off from other people. Remember that emotions and desires are played out mostly through relationships.

You've put up walls between you and those you relate to. These are

the walls of the Tower. You can't get too close to your daughter, she'll want too much from you, too much of your time. You need to break down the walls, to be who you are when you are together. You need to have that insight, suddenly to see any wall you've put up, any way you've held yourself away from somebody so precious, so important, because you had to be this or that.

And when you get down to that bedrock (which is symbolized by nudity in the Tarot), there's nothing more to hide. You begin to reveal who you really are. Remember the star from the Hermit card? Here it is in the Star card. You look down into the pool. The walls have shattered around you, your clothes have burned away, you wake in the still of the night. You see the stars overhead, you look into the pool and see that you are the star that you were following in the Hermit card. And you see your own truth—that you and the stars in that pool are the same.

You'll notice that this is not the last card. You still have some trials to go through. Many of us have had enlightenment experiences, where in a moment we saw the connection between ourselves and the universe. We recognized ourselves as stars. We saw our truth and our purity. But it's not over yet because we still have tasks to do. This gives you hope as you enter the Moon card. You plunge deep into your unconscious to begin dealing with all the debris on the bottom of your pool. No matter what creature is painted on the Moon card, it is always a crustacean. Crustaceans are debris eaters, scavengers, and that's what you have to do. You

have to plunge deep down into your memories, into your unconscious and go through them. A lot of that does not have to be done in the conscious, rational world. It can be done through guided visualization and dreams. That's why this is a nighttime card—the Moon. You can program yourself before you go to sleep or when you're working on these things in therapy or through Tarot counseling.

Often as you begin such processing, reconciliations take place in the dream state. Paul Foster Case says that actual cellular changes occur when you do that. You meet your animal instincts, go through the gateway of technology and all the man-made things to the height of your aspirations, and the sun is born in the Sun card. Here you come out again naked, completely revealed, having become conscious and aware of who you really are.

The Judgement card has more figures on it than any other Major Arcana card. There are many background figures raising their arms, as well as foreground ones. It reminds me of the Parent, Adult, and Child in Transactional Analysis. All the parts of yourself are rising up to a new calling, which is the realization of how your desires led you to your goal—integration with others. As you become more aware of your role and the pure truth and your ability to be in touch with it, a global change occurs.

Judgement is not just for you—it is for everyone on this planet. Until the whole planet is healed there will be no final judgment. As long as one is lost, all is not gained. The ideal is that we all be united as one. Finally in the World card, you see your multidimensional self, who realizes that you

can now dance on what you formerly perceived as your limitations. What you saw as conflicts, fears, and anxieties, you now see as the connecting link. This becomes the form through which you can create. You create through what you are attracted to and repulsed by.

Finally, you reach the resolution, the Universe card, the integration which is what making yourself whole or healing yourself is really about. It's reconciling all the opposites, the dichotomies, the feelings of duality, into a sense of the unity of one, out of which you can then create. From that you break through all your former patterns and bring the opposites together.

When you are working with your own emotions and pain, when you are feeling hurt, angry, and lonely, one of the ways to work through that is to take your cards and place them face up. Then go through them quickly and pick out all the cards that describe exactly how you feel. Just do it without thinking—don't try to reason it out. I make a big pile of all the cards that may express how I feel and all the ones that definitly don't. Then I go through the possible pile and narrow it down; I keep narrowing it down until I have about three to five cards that describe best how I am feeling. Then I write what those cards say about my emotions. When you do this, note what suits are there. See what similarities there are among the cards, and what differences. Often you will find that you weren't feeling what you thought you were feeling—it was something else, something deeper. Then go through the cards and pick out a card that represents how you would like to feel.

You can also describe in cards your ideal state—where you eventually want to be. Then make a path of cards from where you are now to your ideal. Don't be afraid to select cards that show problems along the way. Just include other cards that will help you move through those problems. Find your first step—something concrete—and take it. I notice that by the time I complete such a process, many of the intermediate steps have taken care of themselves. So these can be both interesting and useful ways of working to heal emotional pain by using the Tarot.

AMBER JAYANTI

A Guided Tour of the Qabalistic Tree of Life

Here is an invocation from the Judeo-Christian Qabalistic tradition that I've been schooled in, and I feel that it encapsulates and makes personal the teachings of the ancient Tarot and Qabalah. It's called "The Pattern on the Trestleboard":

> This is the Truth about the Self:
> All the Power that ever was or will be is here now.
> I, you, we are centers of expression for the
> Primal Will to Good, which eternally creates and
> Sustains the universe.
> Through me, through you, through us,
> its unfailing Wisdom takes form in thought and
> word.
> Filled with Understanding of its perfect law, I am
> guided moment by moment along the path of
> liberation.
> From the exhaustless riches of its Limitless
> Substance, I draw all things needful, both
> spiritual and material.
> I recognize manifestation of the undeviating
> Justice in all the circumstances of my life.

> In all things great and small I see the Beauty of
> the divine expression.
> Living from that Will, supported by its unfailing
> Wisdom and Understanding, mine is the victorious
> life.
> I look forward with confidence to the perfect
> realization of the eternal Splendor of the
> Limitless Light.
> In thought and word and deed, I rest my life from
> day to day upon the sure Foundation of Eternal
> Being.
> The realm of Spirit is embodied in my flesh.

The Tree of Life, like the Tarot cards which spring from it, is multi-leveled. Lately, I've been comparing it to a cosmic computer. We can access some of its files to consider the written and unwritten Qabalah, which the Tree of Life puts into symbolic form. Both can be explored by taking a guided tour of the Tree and by answering some repeatedly asked questions. This will give a clearer understanding of the Tree of Life and the study of it.

The first question that needs to be addressed is, What is the Tree of Life and where does it originate? Genesis 2:8,9 states, "And the Lord God planted a garden eastward in Eden . . . And out of the ground made the Lord God to grow every tree that is pleasant to the sight, and good for food; the tree of life also in the midst of the garden, and the tree of knowledge of good and evil." Qabalah, which is among other things the mystical and allegorical interpretation of the Old Testament, says that the knowledge of good and evil—our moral and ethical codes—is communicated to us by our immediate family, our culture, our religious orientation, and so forth. The Tree of Life, by contrast, is something we must learn about by our individual efforts and life experiences.

The Tree of Life, by the way, is not unique to the Qabalistic tradition. There is the Essene Tree of Life, which many believe to be either its precursor or descendent; the Egyptian Tree; the Mayan Tree of Life; and the Norse counterpart, the Yggdrasil.

Qabalists regard the Tree of Life as a map of the involution and evolution of consciousness (top to bottom illustrates involution, bottom to top shows evolution), a mirror of heaven on earth. As such it depicts the building blocks for all creation. It is a mathematical and diagramatic history of the evolution of spirituality. It is also the path to higher consciousness

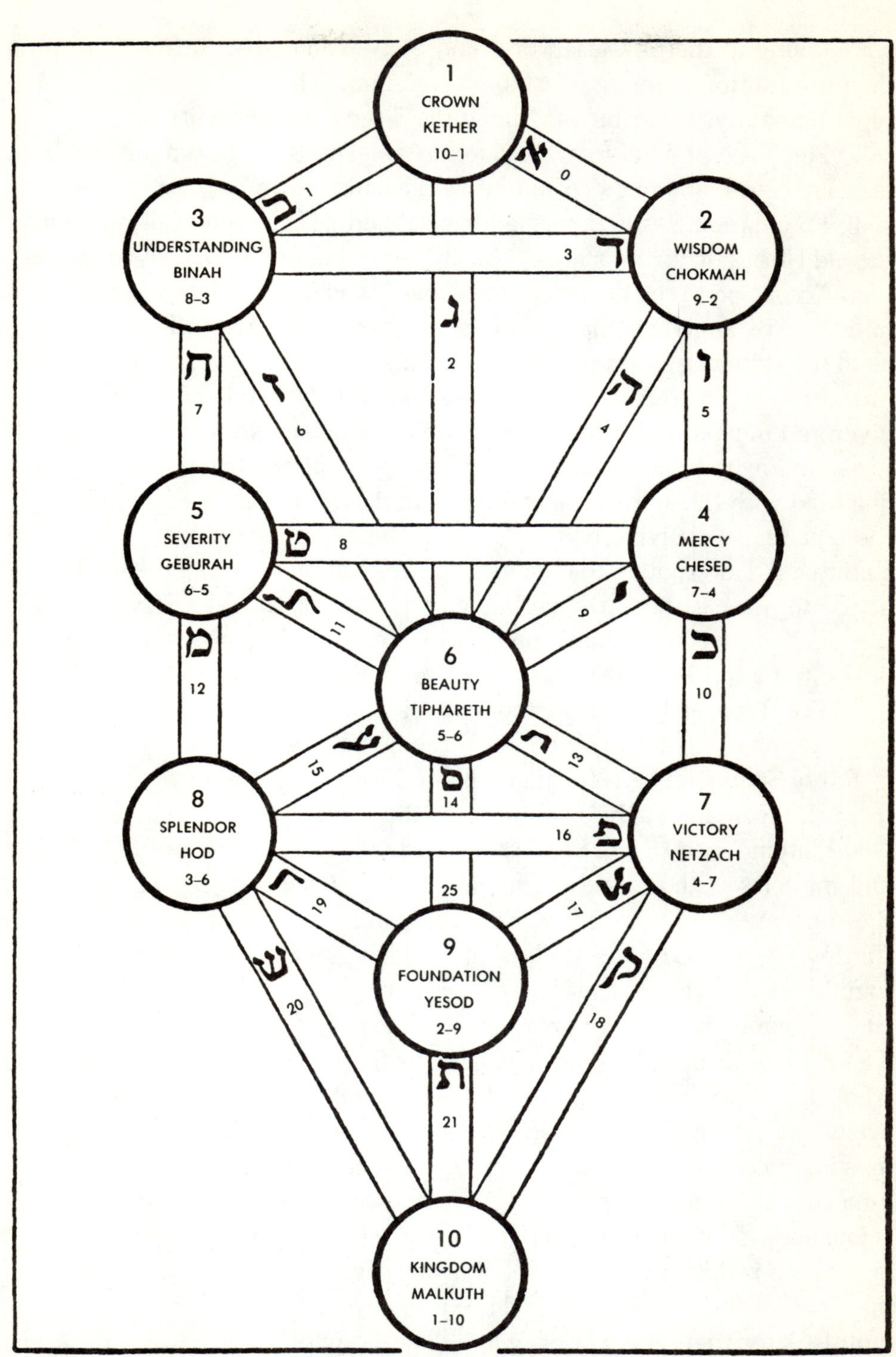

THE TREE OF LIFE

while living in the physical world and body. Aligned with this concept is the presentation of the tree as Adam Kadmon, symbol of generic or archetypal humanity, superimposed upon the Tree from antiquity.

The Tree of Life, then, is also a representation of humanity as both the macrocosm and microcosm (the world-soul, Crown/Kether; the personal soul, Foundation/Yesod; and the physical body, Kingdom/Malkuth). Or as the old Hermetic axiom states, "As above, so below. As below, so above."

According to the ancients, the Qabalah and Tree of Life were given to humanity by angelic beings to bring us consciously back to Eden, to bring us to the state of enlightenment. The translation of the word "Qabalah" is "to gift," or "to receive," rendering the Qabalah and the Tree as gifts given to humankind by the angels. This is an idea which may be difficult for some of us to accept. However, many people who are intimately acquainted with the spiritual world claim that they are inspired or guided by the teachings of Divine beings, such as the channeled works of Seth and Ramtha. An alternative to this, and an explanation which I personally subscribe to, is that these Divine beings are our own Higher Selves coming through because of extended periods of concentration, plus a deep abiding desire to be in touch with this aspect of one's Self.

The Tree of Life also encompasses and represents the mystical interpretation of the first five books of the Old Testament, such as the fruits of Rabbi Schimeon ben Yohai and his son Eleazar's twelve years in hiding from the Romans at the beginning of the second century; the art of the Neo-Platonic Theurgists or miracle workers, who performed both magic and miracles with the aid of angels and benevolent spirits; the works of the thirteenth-century Judeo-Christian Qabalists such as Luria, de Leon, Cordovero, and Lulli; as well as the teachings of the eighteenth-century founder of Chasidism, the Baal Shem Tov.

To paraphrase Dion Fortune in her book, *The Mystical Qabalah* (1935), The Tree of Life, and Tarot, which stems from it, is to the Universal Mind what the dream is to the individual ego, a symbol arising from the subconscious indicating what is hidden. More recently, Paul Foster Case's teachings instructed me that the Tree is a geometrical presentation to the human mind of the interactions that occur between universal and personal consciousness. Of course, it's important to remember that what is perceived is *always* a reflection of the level of awareness of the perceiver. Thus, you may look at the Tree of Life and see it one way, and five weeks later, five months later, five years later, you will see it with another, very different eye. It's a reflection of your level of awareness.

The second main question about the Tree of Life is, What are the Sephiroth and how may I better understand them? The word "Sephiroth" refers to all ten circles, or spheres, on the Tree of Life, while the term "Sephirah" refers to each one individually. The root of these words translates literally from the Hebrew to mean "a shining jewel or emanation."

PRONUNCIATION OF NAMES OF THE SEPHIROTH ON THE TREE OF LIFE

CROWN/KETHER	KETH·ER'	Keth-**er**
WISDOM/CHOKMAH	CHOK·MAH'	Hohk-**maa**
UNDERSTANDING/BINAH	BI·NAH'	Bee-**naa**
MERCY/CHESED	CHE·SED'	Heh-**said**
SEVERITY/GEBURAH	GE·BUR'AH	Geh-**boo**-raa
BEAUTY/TIPHARETH	TIPH·AR'ETH	Tiff-**harr**-eth
VICTORY/NETZACH	NET·ZACH'	Net-**zahk**
SPLENDOR/HOD	HOD	Ha-odd
FOUNDATION/YESOD	YES·OD'	Yes-**odd**
KINGDOM/QUEENDOM/MALKUTH	MAL·KUTH'	Mal-**koo-th**

THE WORD "SEPHIROTH" IS USED WHEN REFERRING TO *ALL* THE SPHERES ON THE TREE OF LIFE AT ONCE.

SEPH·IR·OTH'   Sef-hear-**ohth**

THE WORD "SEPHIRAH" IS USED WHEN REFERRING TO *ONE* OF THE SPHERES ON THE TREE OF LIFE.

SEPH·IR·AH'   Sef-hear-**rah**

Some Qabalists regard the Sephiroth as identical to the Divine Being: each Sephirah represents a different view of the infinite and is in reality God/dess manifest. Others regard the Sephiroth merely as tools or emanations provided by the Most High.

The Sephiroth may symbolize one, that in and through which all change in the universe takes place; and two, that which is unchangeable, the indivisible Yekhidah, or Divine Power. Qabalists term these two different natures of the Sephiroth "Vessels" and "Light," respectively.

Here is a brief description of each Sephirah. The first, Kether, meaning Crown or Exhalted Height, is right on top, number one. It is identical to the one primal will of our Creator/Creatrix. This first Sephirah contains the plan of the universe in its entirety. Many Qabalists don't include Kether among the Sephiroth, since it is not an actual emanation of the Most High, but God/His/Her Self, and they place it at the head of the Sephiroth, regarding it as the Source.

The Tree has three pillars and each represents a segment in time. The Crown/Kether heads the middle one, called the Pillar of Equilibrium or Mildness, and signifies the present. The Crown/Kether stands for the absolute unity which proceeds from the masculine and feminine principles. Wisdom/Chokmah, the Cosmic Father, the highest wisdom, Universal Wisdom, and repository of all human wisdom, heads the Pillar of Mercy and indicates the past. The Pillar of Severity, symbolizing the future, is topped by Understanding/Binah, the Cosmic Mother, giver of the Divine soul to all that lives.

The Union of these two, Wisdom and Understanding, produces Reason or Da'at, the "invisible" Sephirah situated at the point of the Abyss, or gap, between Wisdom and Understanding, which bisects the Middle Pillar. Those who don't include The Crown/Kether among the Sephiroth regard Reason/Da'at as the third Sephirah. But most people consider it a combination of Wisdom and Understanding and not independent.

The first three Sephiroth form the Supernal, Divine, or Super-Conscious Triad or triangle. Since this grouping encompasses the forces of the Universal Mind which create the substance of the universe, it is called the Intellectual Trinity.

The Universal Mind in its threefold manifestation produces the contrasting principles of Mercy/Chesed and Severity/Geburah. The concepts of Mercy and Severity, however, must not be taken completely in their literal sense, but as symbolic designations for the permissive and corrective, expansive and contractive aspects of the One Will. The sum of both, Moral Order, appears as Beauty or Tiphareth. These three Sephiroth compose the Moral, Sensible, or Conscious Triad, the forces in charge of governing the life evolving around it.

The final trinity of the Sephiroth, Victory, Splendor, and Foundation, is considered to be a mirror image of the second triangle and is referred to as the Magical, Astral, or Subconscious Triad, the "stuff" from which the physical world is made. Victory/Netzach is associated with our emotions and imagination plus the desire to live out our dreams and aspirations. Splendor/Hod is the mental planning and organization through which we accomplish our goals. Foundation/Yesod is the Sephirah where all the pre-material forms of the physical world reside and are incorporated into the patterns for completed form.

The tenth Sephirah, at the bottom, Kingdom/Queendom/Malkuth, is the arena in which all the forces from above become manifest. As the material world and body, it is the sum of the activities of all the preceeding Sephiroth. To paraphrase Paul Foster Case, the realm of Spirit is embodied in my flesh, implying that we and our surroundings are in truth reflections or emanations of the one Self, the Crown/Kether.

Another frequent question is, Why do you spell Qabalah with the letter Q, rather than with a C or K, as it's commonly seen? This is simply because in the original Hebrew the word begins with the letter Q, Qoph, not C or K.

One of the more complex questions is, How do the four Qabalistic worlds relate to the Tarot? The four Qabalistic worlds are represented by the four tools on the Magician's table and by the Tetragrammaton, YHWH—Yod, Heh, Vav, Heh—the four-lettered name of the Most High that appears in several places in most Tarot decks, most commonly around the Wheel of Fortune.

The first world starts at the top of the Tree. It is the World of Archetypes, The Divine World, Atziluth, and corresponds to the first letter of the Tetragrammaton, Yod, the wand on the Magician's table, and subsequently, the element of fire. This almost inexplicable world of the higher mind is associated with the Divine spark of life, inspiration, and the outward and downward flux of emanations from above. Scientifically it may be equated with the realm of atoms and electrons. This world includes the Supernal Triangle of Crown, Wisdom, and Understanding.

The second world is that of Briah, the World of Creation. It's attributed to the first Heh in the Tetragrammaton, the water element, and the cup on the Magician's table. It is associated with creative potential, imagination, and feelings. Briah is scientifically linked to the gaseous state. This world includes the Moral Triad of Mercy, Severity, and Beauty.

The third Qabalistic world is the World of Formation, Yetzirah. We can have all the good ideas and creative potential in the world, but unless we are willing to *act*, to consciously commit ourselves to what we want to manifest, our ideas and imaginings will bear the fruits of chance, not

Qabalistic Worlds
of the Tetragrammaton
יהוה

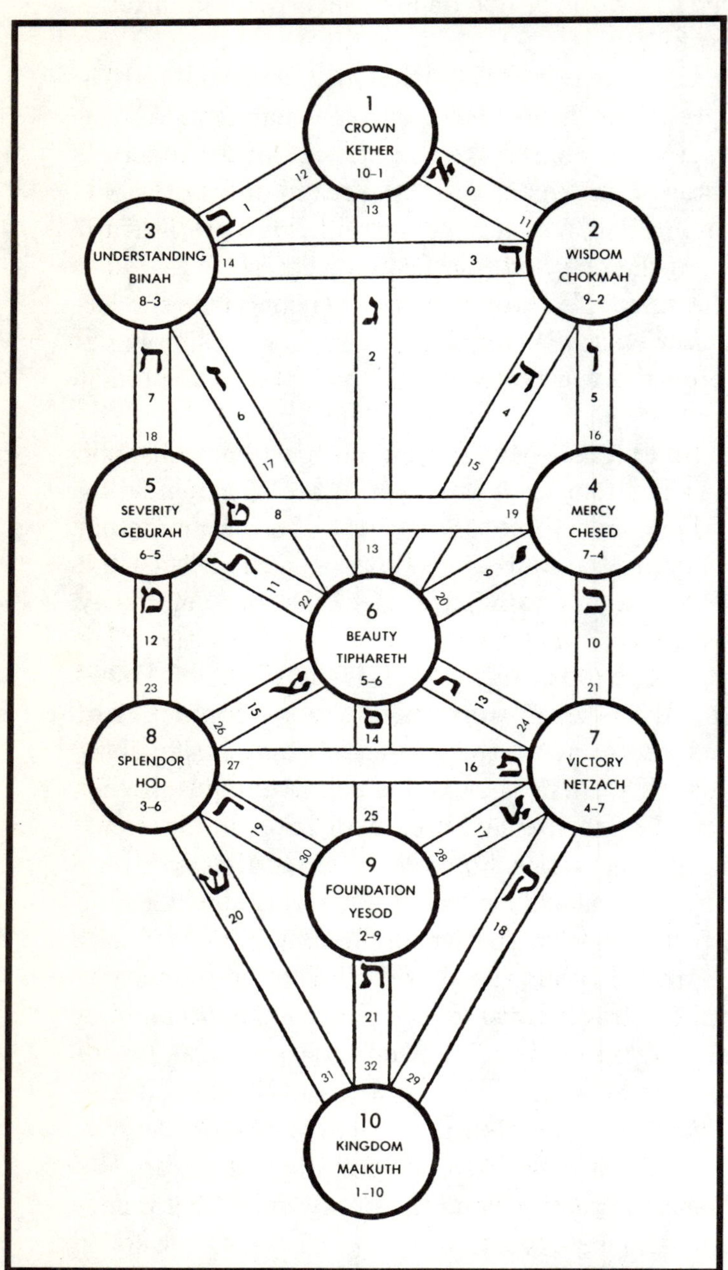

Atziluth   י Yod
Molecules
Archetypal World
Kether, Chokmah, Binah

Briah   ה Heh
Gases
Creative World
Chesed, Geburah,
Tiphareth

Yetzirah   ו Vav
Liquids
Formative World
Netzach, Hod, Yesod

Assiah   ה Heh
Solids
Manifest World
Malkuth

choice. Consequently, this plane is associated with the sword, and all that goes with it, the cutting away of extraneous material in order to make decisions, discriminate, sort, set limits, etc. This world is aligned with the air element and the Hebrew letter Vav, meaning "link," from the Tetragrammaton, as the World of Formation is what inevitably links the invisible and visible worlds. It includes Yetzirah, the Astral or Magical Triad of Victory, Splendor, and Foundation, and may be linked to the liquid state.

The fourth and final world, Assiah, the World of Manifestation, is the Magician's pentacle, the completed product or finished works, the physical world and body, the element of earth and the final Heh in the name of the Most High. It is the birth of what was conceived in the three other worlds above and as such contains the product of our inspirations, thoughts, creative yearnings, and actions.

Another frequent question is whether the Tree of Life can help in understanding the soul's three aspects, Neshemah, Ruach, and Nefesh. It definitely can. It's useful to approach this question from two different perspectives.

First, Nefesh, which resides in Foundation, also termed the Anima Mundi or world soul, contains the astral and etheric vehicles, the matrix for the physical body. Ruach, the next level, encompasses the conscious personality or individuality and is seated in Beauty. The highest level of the soul, Neshemah, the vessel which holds our spiritual nature, the Divine soul which the Most High wishes us to have, dwells in Understanding.

As another way of explaining these three levels more concretely, the glassblower is the Divine soul, Neshemah, situated in Understanding. The tube that carries the Divine breath or spirit to the Higher Self, and to the physical Vessel, is Ruach, situated in Beauty. The Vessel being created is Nefesh, in Foundation.

Another question is, Who is Adam Kadmon? The Qabalists have used the symbol of generic or archetypal humanity, Adam Kadmon, to represent the Tree of Life for countless generations. It is the Tree of Life in Human form, and a simple way of stating both that we are the Tree of Life and that we are Divine.

It's interesting to note that although the Hebrew word "Adam" means "Man," it is derived from the same root as the feminine word "Adamah," meaning "mother earth." This is depicted as a half-male, half-female body, upon which the Qabalist's seven "Inner Stars," the Western counterpart of the East's chakra system, are aligned with the ten Sephiroth from the Tree of Life.

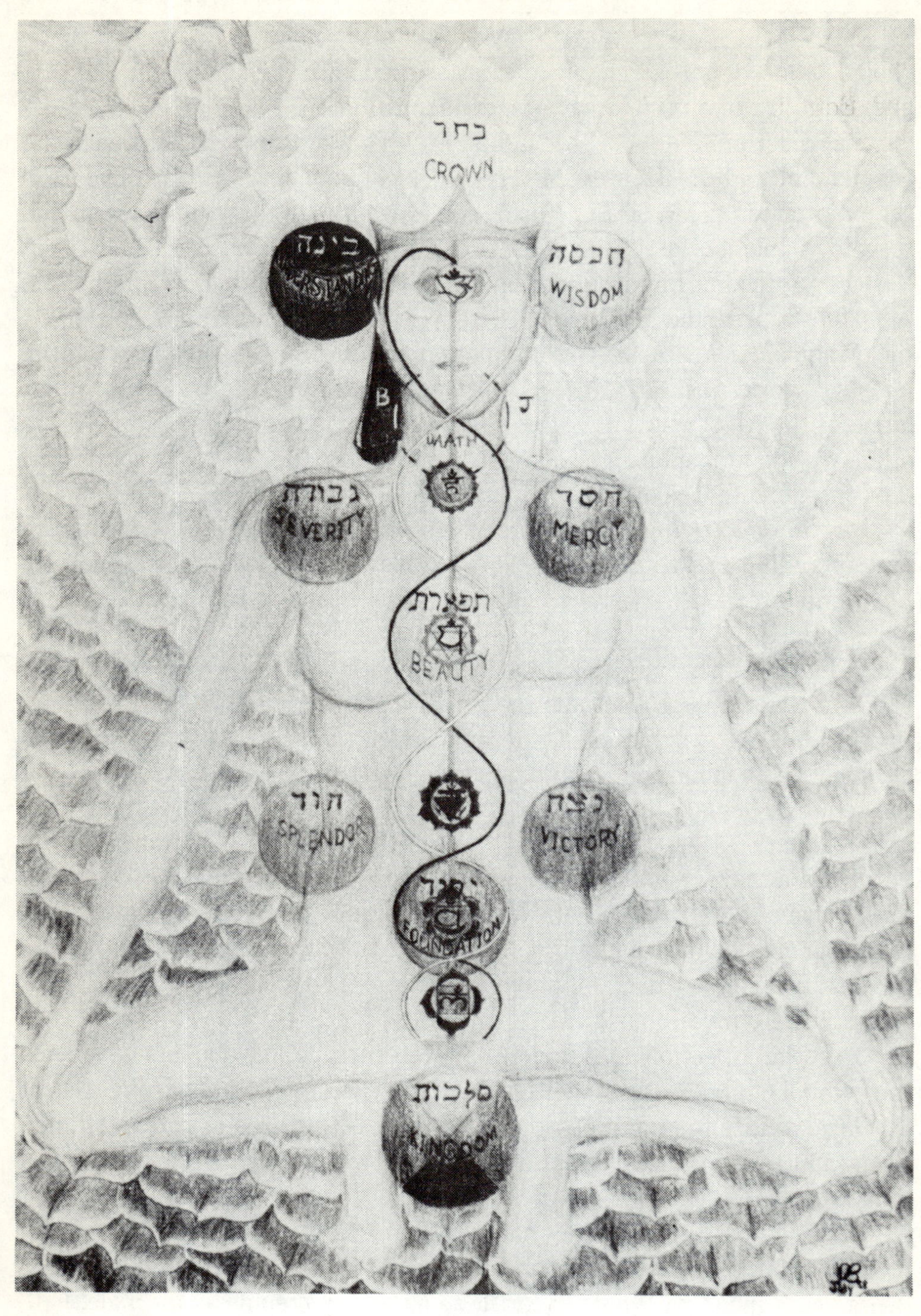
כתר
CROWN
בינה
UNDERSTANDING
חכמה
WISDOM
B
J
DAATH
גבורה
SEVERITY
חסד
MERCY
תפארת
BEAUTY
הוד
SPLENDOR
נצח
VICTORY
יסוד
FOUNDATION
מלכות
KINGDOM

As we know, the Tree has three pillars, those of Mercy, Severity, and Equilibrium. Facing the Tree, these correspond in the spine to the Yogic Pingala, the positive right male channel, the Ida, the negative left female channel, and the Shushuma, the neutral central channel. The Holy Spirit, or Kundalini energy within, spirals up and down the spine, in and through the seven Inner Stars.

Because The Crown signifies union with God/dess and symbolizes the place from which the body, in fact all bodies, originates, it's most often called "the Beginning of the Whirlings." It corresponds to the Crown Center, which Yogis call the Sahasrar, or thousand-petaled lotus, our connection with the Infinite.

Wisdom/Chokmah, the Supernal Father, corresponds to the left side of the face and left brain. Understanding/Briah, the Supernal Mother, is attributed to the right side of the face and right brain. These, our intellect and intuition respectively, are linked to the Third or Inner Eye.

Next we have Reason/Da'at, the invisible Sephirah which links the head, or mind, to the body. It's correlated to the neck and the Throat Center, seat of creative self-expression, or our voice in the world.

In this same latitude reside Mercy/Chesed, the permissive left arm, and Severity/Geburah, the right arm. Mercy/Chesed extends consciously throughout the body, stimulating compassion, forgiveness, and loving protection. Severity/Geburah, or "The Enforcer," whose job it is to rectify what is not aligned with the Greatest Good, takes a neutral stand. It sees what needs to be done and does it, without judgment or attachment.

Beauty/Tiphareth resides in the middle of the chest, the Heart Center, seat of the Mesheach, or Redeemer, unconditional love.

Linked to the Solar Plexus Center are Victory/Netzach and Splendor/Hod, the left and right hips and legs respectively, indicating how we, the ego or personality, instinctively seek to assert our way through life to meet our destiny.

Foundation/Yesod corresponds to the Reproductive Center, the male and female sex glands and organs, as well as to the astral body. It is the place where the drive to reproduce ourselves and manifest our dreams is situated.

Finally, Kingdom/Malkuth, the feet and anus, is aligned with the Root Center, signifying survival skills, or just how solidly our feet are on the ground.

Here's another question that's often voiced: I've heard that there are thirty-two paths, but I see only twenty-two. Where are the remaining ten?

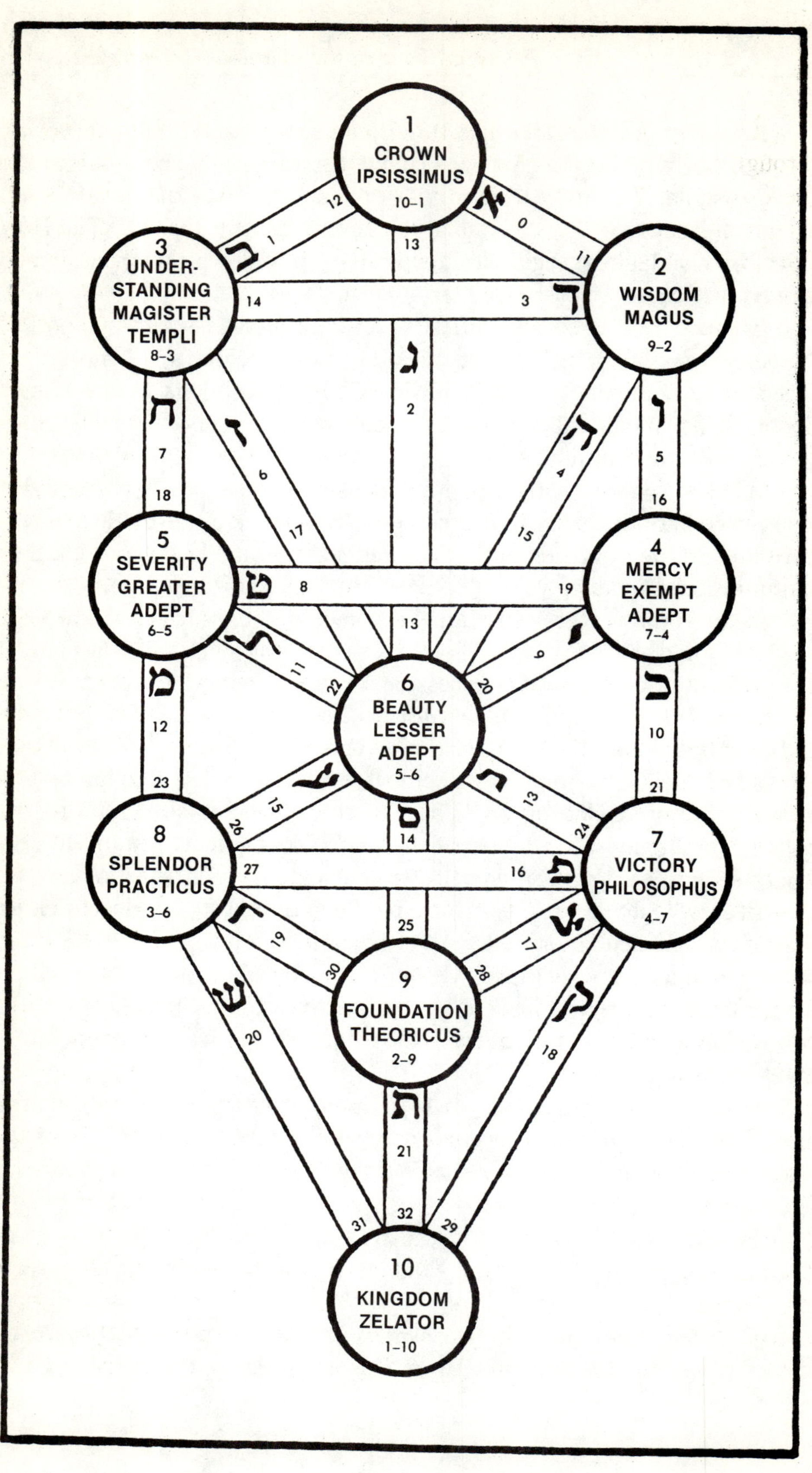

1
CROWN
IPSISSIMUS
10–1
3
UNDER-
STANDING
MAGISTER
TEMPLI
8–3
2
WISDOM
MAGUS
9–2
5
SEVERITY
GREATER
ADEPT
6–5
4
MERCY
EXEMPT
ADEPT
7–4
6
BEAUTY
LESSER
ADEPT
5–6
8
SPLENDOR
PRACTICUS
3–6
7
VICTORY
PHILOSOPHUS
4–7
9
FOUNDATION
THEORICUS
2–9
10
KINGDOM
ZELATOR
1–10

The Sephiroth themselves are the first ten paths, numbered one through ten. The number on the Fool's path or channel running between the Crown and Wisdom, eleven, confirms this. Qabalistic tradition has a system of grades or degrees like those used in the Masonic and Rosicrucian Orders, as all three are believed to have the same origin. This system of grades, levels, or classifications of spiritual development is based upon our ascent up the Tree of Life. This will be discussed more fully in my next book, *Qabalah for the 21st Century*.

Students of astrology ask, Since all the planets are included in the paths (the channels between the Sephiroth), why do the first seven appear again in the Sephiroth? Qabalistic astrologers call the planets the seven Internal Stars—the energy centers or chakras. They report that these function *within* the individual like the planets in the heavens. This brand of astrology is essentially a belief in the Law of Synchronicity, recently parented by the budding science of sub-atomic physics, which states, "All events are tied together in an unbroken wholeness." Macrocosm reflects microcosm.

As you've seen on the Tree of Life, the twenty-two Major Arcana cards, each of which is also an astrological sign or planet, are on the paths between the Sephiroth. As such, they denote the Universal Laws and principles or heavenly guidelines for life here on earth. This suggests that the paths indicate the external function of a planet, its place in the greater scheme of things. The Sephiroth represent the planet's inner operation, the way the planet operates within the human personality. Hence the twin appearance of the first seven planets, and via the Law of Synchronicity, the way in which the movement of the planets have a naturally meaningful relationship to events here on earth.

The all-embracing question at this point is, How can I connect, corrolate, begin to merge the Tarot with the Tree of Life? There comes a time when we want to know more about the Tree of Life, to have a personal experience of it; of course, the place to find this information is within our own lives and consciousness. This is where the Tarot genuinely begins to come together with the Tree of Life.

In the tradition that I was trained in, the Tarot cards are called "Keys." Initially I was puzzled by this, but in time I realized that they are the Keys to unlock the doors of Higher Consciousness. I was taught that the "Keys" symbolize the Universal Laws and Principles of Life, and that these "Keys" may be used to unlock the mysteries of the various Sephiroth. It is interesting to note that the Sephiroth are sometimes called

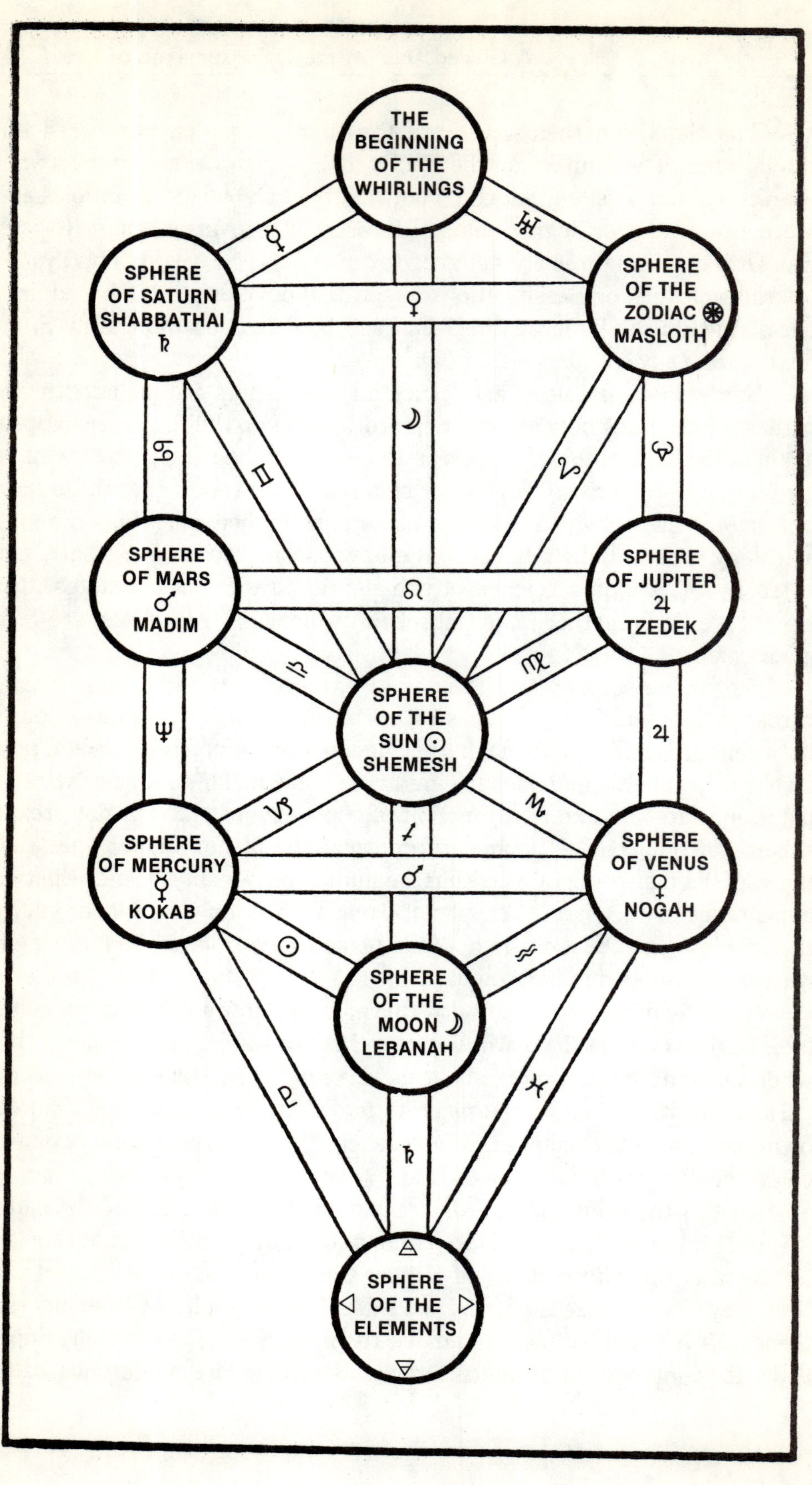

THE BEGINNING OF THE WHIRLINGS
SPHERE OF SATURN SHABBATHAI
SPHERE OF THE ZODIAC MASLOTH
SPHERE OF MARS MADIM
SPHERE OF JUPITER TZEDEK
SPHERE OF THE SUN SHEMESH
SPHERE OF MERCURY KOKAB
SPHERE OF VENUS NOGAH
SPHERE OF THE MOON LEBANAH
SPHERE OF THE ELEMENTS

"Gates." In order to work your way along the path to higher Consciousness on the Tree of Life, it is essential to have an in-depth working knowledge of the Keys, the impersonal Universal Laws and Principles. These are the means or "paths" to higher consciousness. In other words, each Sephirah represents a step in our personal evolution; without having a "working" set of Keys, the Gates cannot be opened.

As we've seen, the Knowledge of Good and Evil, our morals, are communicated to us by our family, culture, and the like. I see that the Tarot and its impersonal wisdom, or for that matter the teachings of whatever spiritual path you're on, are also analogous to the Tree of Knowledge. It is by taking this impersonal wisdom to heart and using it in our daily life that we climb the Tree of Life.

In a very practical sense, how can we use the universal teachings of the Tarot to help us understand and meet the challenges of everyday living to the best of our ability? Here's an example: I teach a class called "Eclectic Meditation," and at one point I decided that since experience is such a great teacher, I would take a group of students to a beautiful yet remote Zen monastery, to acquaint them firsthand with the practice of Zen. It took a lot of preparation. We had to plan months and months in advance.

Finally, the morning of the departure came, and I was feeling more than a bit over-responsible for everyone—what clothes to bring, what to sit on, the temperature, and so on. And I said to myself, All right, quiet down. I knew it would be good medicine to turn to the Tarot. So I picked up my cards and after asking my Higher Self for guidance, turned over the Sun card. And soon I began to understand how I could get over my worries—the wall that I had constructed for myself about how others would adjust to the unfamiliar surroundings and somewhat stringent routine. I could get over this wall very simply by following the light, by enthusiastically getting involved in the workings of the monastery as I had in the past, on other visits without an entourage. I could forget that I had all these people with me. I could even set a good nonverbal example for them to follow. I would get up at five o'clock for meditation; I would participate in the prescribed routine; I would do the service that was expected of me while I was there.

Next, I looked at the Tree of Life and saw that the Sun's path runs between Splendor and Foundation, the intellect and the subconscious, respectively. So I figured out that by willfully turning down my excessive emotions (Victory) and involving myself in the act of disciplining and balancing my thoughts and actions (Splendor), I could set the best example possible for my students. Not only would they probably follow my example, but as an added benefit, I would be altering a pattern in the foundation of my own personality—that of assuming over-responsibility for others who are perfectly capable of caring for themselves. By doing this, I would be deriving my sustenance and support from the Source, from the Sun, and letting that light shine through me, rather than having my behavior run by a worthless habit.

In summary, the Tree of Life is a cosmic computer—a huge memory bank of theological, theosophical, metaphysical, philosophical, scientific, astrological, and psychological wisdom. The Tree of Life and the Qabalah, and the Tarot they equate to, are a living, growing, constantly transforming system and philosophy. And if we take the time and effort to focus on this system, the inexplicable becomes apparent.

WILLIAM C. LAMMEY

What Is Karmic Tarot?

THE TAROT IS AN EXCELLENT AND FRIENDLY introduction to metaphysics in general, because it embodies so many of the underlying mysteries in our universe. And once the Tarot has picked you as one of its students, you're on a life path of continual enlightenment through the largesse of this in-house best friend and advisor, this counselor that you can keep in a box.

I know that the Tarot picked me. It somehow spotted me and told me that I was going to buy that first deck. I think that is what really happens to every person who is interested in the Tarot. Somehow you're picked and then you spend the rest of your life figuring out why and what you're supposed to do with Tarot, what it really is and how to be smarter about it.

I'd like to point out that all my references to Tarot are based on what I call the classical Tarot. That's my way of referring to any seventy-eight-card deck that has a twenty-two-card Major Arcana and a fifty-six-card Minor Arcana. The basis of my book, *Karmic Tarot*, really came from the realization that those numbers are very, very important. The twenty-two cards of the Major Arcana *really mean something*. The fact that there are four suits in the Minor Arcana *really means something*. And the fact that there are ten Pip cards—ten numbered cards—not nine, not eleven—*ten*. And the fact that the Court Cards are four.

I kept thinking about those simple things. I kept saying to myself, Why twenty-two? Why twenty-two? What are the patterns in there? In the numerology that's underneath all of Tarot, there is a kind of basic symbology. In studying the Tarot, take your investigation of the deck back to the simplest idea of each individual card that you can force yourself into. Try to reduce it to a single essence, because that's what it is. The Three of Pentacles is the Three of Pentacles. It's everything that a pentacle is and it's everything that a three is. No matter how many meanings may come to you for this card, all of those meanings will derive from this simple essence. In any case, just know that when I refer to the classical Tarot, I'm speaking about any seventy-eight-card deck.

Everything that happens in our daily lives is part of the unfolding of the divine purpose of our chosen life path. The more we're able to grasp the essence of that purpose, the more harmonious that unfolding will be. The Tarot is a system that enables our intuitive soul, our spirit self, to communicate with our objective mind, emotions and body. There is unlimited information available to us from the intuitive level, and the Tarot is an excellent way of externalizing that inner information, of getting it outside ourselves, where we can work with it.

The Tarot has a great deal to offer for other fields of study as well, because it is both a rational and an intuitive system. That is its special value. It straddles the fence. As such, it's an extraordinary blend of right- and left-brain thinking. In fact, Tarot is a left-brain system for interpreting right-brain, intuitive information. It's a device at the mental level for organizing input from the spiritual level. It is a rational system of archetypal symbols and structured layouts on which the intuitive right brain can play its half of the game. And as such, it's an excellent tool for exercising and training the brain. Tarot is a gift from God to help us on the path, to help us make our future, not to tell us what our future will be. In a sense it's a little like the mechanics of Dickens's Scrooge: it shows us what can be, like an early warning system; but like Scrooge, we can change. I fully believe that Tarot was conceived as a tool to aid man in fulfilling his divine purpose. There's no doubt in my mind that the knowledge of the Tarot can improve our lives and the lives of the people for whom we read.

The historic origins of the Tarot are not strategic to a discussion of Karmic Tarot. But the origins of Tarot in terms of its purpose are strategic. In looking at Tarot intensely and from many viewpoints, we see the underlying principles, structure and patterns that are at work. Most importantly, we recognize that the Tarot is both a living language and, in the sense of visual symbols, a written language. In fact, it may well be among the oldest of all written languages, even in spite of the fact that the oldest deck known today is from the fifteenth century. It is actually a partial deck of seventeen cards, generally believed to have been made by Gringonneur for Charles VI. There's also another theory that the Tarot is Italian, dating from around 1470. In any case, these seventeen cards, now in the Bibliothèque Nationale in Paris, are the earliest known physical Tarot cards.

Tarot symbology could well have been born at that magic ancient moment when man invented the first alphabet to capture visually the sounds of speech. This, in fact, was the moment when symbology itself was born. This is the original stuff from which archetypes themselves derive. Man's ability to communicate through the sense of sight, what I refer to as the "mental plane," was born. The reason archetypal symbology moves us in such a deep and mysterious way is that it's prelingual and premental. Even now it is hard to express many of these messages in words.

Much of the work with the Tarot has been limited to future forecasting. It has been placed side by side with mediums used primarily for fortune telling, such as palmistry, tea leaves and crystal balls. The more serious work from correlations with the Hebrew alphabet and the Qabalah, astrology and the various mythologies has centered around the twenty-two cards of the Major Arcana. And even when the emphasis of such work has been on looking at the Major Arcana as a pathway in the evolution of consciousness, the end result has been little more than enriched meanings for the twenty-two cards.

In Karmic Tarot we see how the Minor as well as the Major Arcana are used to define that path. A structure within each of the Arcana, as well as a structural relationship between the two, is uncovered and a wealth of new information is revealed, producing a new spread, the Karmic Spread, and expanded meaning for all seventy-eight cards, not just the Major Arcana. It stimulates the generation of personal meanings for each reader and facilitates remembering. The Karmic Spread reflects our evolution of consciousness as a journey that the four-fold self takes through the seven stages of evolutionary consciousness. These four aspects of the self are the physical, emotional, mental, and spiritual levels. The seven stages that appear in the spread enable us to relate the Tarot to the growing knowledge of the underlying similarity and harmony between Eastern and Western philosophies. For example, the significance of the stages correlate to the seven chakras in the unfolding of the Kundalini, as used by yogis. The same seven stages of consciousness are referred to by transpersonal psychologists. These are all aspects of the same thing.

The names "Karmic Tarot" and "Karmic Spread" derive from the first stage's representation of our situation at the moment of our incarnation. This stage is in effect our Karmic contract at the time of our birth. It provides information about what we have chosen to do in this lifetime. The information given will be the aspects of the birth contract that relate to the main message of that particular reading.

In Karmic Tarot we also begin to see how each Arcana can be used to deepen our understanding of the meaning of the cards in the other Arcana —much as words in the dictionary send you endlessly back and forth, but with increasingly better definitions. Just as we use words to define words in conventional language, we can use cards to define cards in the language of the Tarot. And this is very important in interpreting the Minor Arcana. Our understanding of, and our ability to use, the Tarot as a guide for ourselves is enhanced by the revelation of this new information. The more we can see into the mechanics behind and within the Tarot, the less we will depend on blind memorization of cards and arbitrary layouts, and the more we will see where each card fits into the whole. Once we see the fit, the mind will automatically fill up with interpretations.

Karmic Tarot uses the rich philosophical treasures inherent in the concepts of reincarnation and Karma as a means of discerning aspects of the Karmic purpose chosen by the soul at birth. But it is also a highly pragmatic system for seeing that purpose at work in our day-to-day affairs. It enables us to gather, in very specific time frames, rich information about the pragmatic issues in our current life situation. Every question, no matter how simple or complex, is considered in the overall context of the underlying framework of the present lifetime. The Karmic Tarot is looking hard for the underlying principles, the patterns that are at work, the lessons of the structure of the Tarot itself, to guide the reader and kindle the knowledge hidden deep within each of us as readers with potentially great skill. With Karmic Tarot there's no need to laboriously memorize meanings for the cards. The Tarot itself will teach each reader what the correct meanings are for them. When we allow the essence of the cards to speak directly to us, observe their relationships in the deck and observe the organization and structure in the deck, the meanings will always be there when we need them. They will bubble up from deep inside us during the reading with little or no conscious effort.

Most people interested in metaphysics and in the Tarot in particular believe in the concepts of reincarnation and Karma. My working definition of reincarnation, which underlies Karmic Tarot, is the belief that the essence of our being, the soul, never dies and is reborn materially in new bodies in a series of lifetimes, as our consciousness evolves from the very separateness of man to the very oneness of the divine.

My definition of Karma is the belief that the soul's agenda for a given lifetime is determined by the progress we make on our path of evolving consciousness. Please notice that there is nothing remotely suggestive of anything negative in this definition of Karma. The popular concept of Karma as negative is fundamentally wrong. Many people think in terms of having to make up for what we have done in our past lives, as if there were some sort of Karmic yoke carried in each incarnation. This negative slant is inaccurate and in my opinion, it's bad metaphysics. It suggests that we begin our lives with handicaps. But we do not begin life with any punishment for poor past performances, any more than we begin with any advantages for good performances. God does not punish before, during or after the lifetime. All negativity and pain are simply part of the process whereby we choose and learn our lessons on the path.

Every lifetime for every soul begins on an even keel. But the soul knows from its own vantage point what it needs to do and it will always choose hard work. The soul will always choose its agenda for the present lifetime with full knowledge and complete understanding of its record to date. It will therefore choose an identity and task that will take into consideration its progress to date—and the progress to date is the result of all the past action. From the overview available to the soul, it will choose what it needs to accomplish to best further its progress on the path, which is the evolution of its consciousness. And to the soul, to the God "within" and to the God "without," no identity and no task is any better or any worse than any other. It is simply a question of what is the best choice for making progress.

God is everything from the infinitely small to the infinitely large. When the focus is on the God without, as it is in most organized religion, in particular for fundamentalists, the individual personality identifies with the aspect of the divine which is seen to exist externally to them. This is the "masculine" side of God, the all-powerful, all-capable judgmental side of the divine. At its extreme it represents the infinitely large in the universe. When the focus is on the God within, as it is in most New Age disciplines, the aspect of the divine with which the individual personality identifies is that seen to exist deep inside each of us. It is the "feminine" side of God that lives here—the benevolent, understanding, forgiving side of the divine. At its extreme it represents the infinitely small in the universe.

Fundamental to the concept of a discernable Karma at work in the Tarot is the belief that each of us, as the soul is preparing to be born, to incarnate, decides on a master plan for the lifetime ahead. For all intents and purposes this is a contract, an outline, a framework agreed upon with God. In a sense we can say that at this point the God within agrees on a framework with the God without. The degree to which we satisfy this contract is the degree to which we will be happy and successful. In other words, we feel fulfilled when we are fulfilling our contract. This is the Karmic Contract. We feel most angry when we're not meeting the terms of our contract because we're violating an agreement we've made with ourselves. Prior to birth, free will is expressed by the choices of our soul for the framework of the path. After our birth, free will is expressed by the way in which we choose to fill in that framework. And we have an apparent infinity of choices within the agreed-upon framework.

The God within and the God without, yourself and God, the soul—we are choosing the goals, the parameters. And in Karmic Tarot, we see the four aspects of those choices at the beginning of the spread. It's as if we choose to build a tower, and we select the four columns for the corners—the structural framework and the foundation of our tower. The four columns represent the physical, emotional, mental, and spiritual aspects of the lifetime to come. And while we cannot go outside the parameters of our tower, we can build it as high as we want, and we can fill it as we please. In fact, that is just what we're supposed to do. By following our parameters and using the structure of our tower, we can reach the heavens.

We are born with complete knowledge of our Karmic Contract, and our challenge in the game of life, if you will, in the task of being human, is to see how efficiently we can bring the lessons contained in that intuitive knowledge into fruition in our conscious existence. God communicates with us continuously to remind us of the timely, pressing requirements of our contract. A centered life path is one very much on target with the soul's obligation, one that is "getting the message." These are the people whose lives seem charmed, people who always appear to be happy, healthy, and of course, extremely lucky. We just want to slap them silly. These are the people who test us via the sin of envy. Using the Tower analogy, we want to stay centered in the middle of our tower, paying equal and full attention to all four corners.

God communicates with all of us equally, but we do not listen equally, with equal attention. Centered people are, by definition, good listeners.

Those of us who are not very centered, who are less than perfect listeners, must be reached in more concrete ways. And these ways are on a sliding scale from minor to major attention getters. Initially, the reminders are internal—in our heads. We are first given the opportunity to learn our lessons at the spiritual level. Lessons learned at the spiritual level have no pain or negativity, since the lesson is internalized so quickly. The wise ones sitting on mountain tops and in the caves in the Himalayas are learning almost all, if not all, of their lessons at the spiritual level. You can almost see the lessons clicking into their consciousness as you look into their eyes. If, however, the lesson is not learned at the spiritual level, it will drop to the mental level. In other words, it will come into our conscious thoughts slowly at first, through recurring dreams and daydreams. Headaches can even be thought of as information heating up, trying to get out. Headaches are our red telephone to heaven. They are God calling, telling us we should slow down, that there's something He wants us to know, to take cognizance of, something we've been missing. He wants us to stop whatever we're doing, find a quiet corner and listen. And if necessary, the message will be externalized, in the form of unsolicited advice from family and friends, or even the introduction of new people, seemingly out of the blue. If we still don't get the message, and don't learn the lesson at the mental level, it will drop to the emotional level. And if it's not learned there, it will fall to the physical level, where at the extreme we encounter accidents and illnesses. In this descent from the spiritual through the mental and then the emotional to the physical, there is an increasing degree of pain and negativity. We see the importance of this structure in the design of the Minor Arcana, for the four suits of the Minor Arcana represent the experiences in life at these four levels—the spiritual, mental, emotional, and physical.

Now at first this may sound a little funny, but God does not speak English. The Divine does not communicate directly with us in the English language. Language was invented by man to communicate with man. And as studies in the fields of linguistics and linguistic philosophy continue to show, language is fraught with pitfalls. That's why the study of archetypal symbols and mythology is so important. Tarot and language were born out of the same symbology, the same archetypes. When man first felt the need to create visual symbols of his verbal speech, which, by the way, was his first giant step toward conquering time and distance, he created the first alphabets.

Everything is communicating to us all the time. Getting our attention is the name of the game. Then it is part of the nature of being human that we must figure it all out for ourselves, but we are always pointed in the right direction. He leads us to the water but He will not make us drink. This is the message of the painting on the ceiling of the Sistine Chapel, in which the hand and finger of God are reaching out to man's, but they're not quite touching. It requires a leap of faith on the part of man to make the contact and to receive the full effect of the Holy Spirit.

Now I want to say a few things about prayer versus meditation, in relation to the Tarot. The Tarot is symbolic externalization of spiritual-level input from God: the stuff that seems to come in through the top of our heads. However, man, particularly Western man, finds it much easier to work with external input—information that comes in through the five senses. Western man simply has not been conditioned to acknowledge and interpret the sixth sense, the inner voice, very well. We seem either to not listen at all or to listen indiscriminately. Of course with the current impact of Eastern philosophies and practices and with the growth in the popularity of, for example, Tarot, this is rapidly changing.

When Western man turns his attention toward God, he usually does so in the form of prayer. When Eastern man turns toward God, he meditates. In prayer, the major form is interrogatory. We're not just asking questions, we're asking for *things*. But the main thing to note here is that *we're* doing most of the talking. In meditation, the major form is silence—so that we can listen. The Tarot is a form of listening. It's on the good side of the fence. In Tarot the message is externalized in the form of the cards and then taken back in through the senses of sight and sound: sight if you're reading for yourself, sight and sound if you're reading for somebody else. Tarot stops the mind and gives it focus. It provides a means of centering ourselves on the path. It supplies specific course-corrective information. It's an efficient and relatively painless way of getting the message. Tarot is functioning at the mental level. And remember, the message we do not get at the mental level will drop to the emotional and then to the physical.

Usually, in Tarot we are working on solving problems. We may cover a lot of different things but in fact we want to get someplace. It's important to keep in mind that there are no bad cards in the Tarot, only lessons to be learned. And "lessons to be learned" is just a more positive way of saying "problems to be solved." Our lives are really quite simply a series of lessons on our path. That which is flowing and already bringing us joy is the result of lessons already learned, or in the process of being learned. That which is not flowing begins to present itself by definition as a problem, as something negative. This negativity is designed to draw our attention to a lesson we need to learn. The instant that the lesson is learned and internalized, the problem disappears. The problem is no longer a problem.

All of the so-called negative experiences we have are nothing more than lessons to be learned. Acceptance of this fact can be very hard when we're in the midst of intense pain or sorrow. But it's the acceptance that is the first step in converting the illusion of negativity, that very pain and sorrow, into the joy that is rightfully ours on our path. The trick is to consciously assert the fact that in the midst of all the apparent negativity there is indeed something very positive. That positive "something" is the lesson to be learned. The catch-22 is to be able to search for the positive while the negative still has us numb with pain. Negativity draws our attention because we want it to stop, but we're also automatically repelled by it. It's sort of a one-two punch, and we must let it get our attention, but not allow ourselves to be repelled by it after it does. We must hold our attention and our focus on the pain. Somewhere in that pain is the positive lesson to be learned. Upon discovering and then learning the lesson, the problem will be solved. The pain will be dissolved and then the negativity will be gone, forever. Tomorrow's lesson may be worse than today's, but at least today's is gone.

Tarot can save us so much pain. It shows us the lessons we're facing, the potential negativity. If we can learn what lesson that potential problem has for us, learn it in a reading, we no longer need to experience it. We can go on to the next lesson. In other words, we do not need to actually experience any pain, we just need to do our homework and learn our lessons. And this is true, no matter what the Karmic carry-over affecting the soul's choices and the four planes at birth may be. Our first opportunity to learn is at the spiritual level, where the lessons learned carry no pain whatsoever. Our next opportunity comes at the mental level. Remember that Tarot operates at the mental level as a rational left-brain system for interpreting intuitive right-brain information. Lessons learned at the mental level avoid the more painful and negative lessons at the emotional and physical levels. The function of the duality of positive and negative follows that of all dualities, that is, hot/cold, up/down, good/evil, God and the devil. They exist and they don't exist, and we must deal with them in both

KARMIC SPREAD POSITION DEFINITIONS—A SUMMARY

POSITION IN SPREAD	MEANING OF POSITIONS
1 MAGICIAN	Physical package at birth . . . influence of parents esp. Father . . . Part of Karmic Contract. Fears Disposition of physical health . . . our biological package . . . Inheritance (wills) will to live How we approach material things. Our instincts as survival mechanisms . . . Our disposition toward fear/paranoia . . . Our physical safety . . .
2 PRIESTESS	Emotional package at birth . . . Influence of mother . . . Part of Karmic Contract. Passions Disposition of emotional health . . . Attitude toward touch/physical love . . . Toward self/then others will to feel
3 EMPRESS	Mental package at birth . . . IQ . . . Part of Karmic Contract. Concepts Disposition of mental health . . . will to know Mind applied to self preservation . . . Our ability to learn/to analyze . . . begins here . . . at the physical level
4 EMPEROR	Spiritual package at birth . . . Part of Karmic Contract . . . Key card of the four Contract Cards. Faith Our spiritual "health" . . . will to will/to believe How we begin things . . . Our approach . . . Our style End of Stage One: Physical . . . Beginning of Stage Two: Emotional
5 HIEROPHANT	Our earliest philosophy/ideology package . . . The system(s) of thought that we are born into . . . Mental impact of early environment . . . Earliest effect of feelings on thought . . . The ego begins to develop . . . and as we begin to see ourselves, we begin to see others . . . The dawn of duality in our consciousness . . . The birth of conscience.
6 LOVERS	Emotional impact of early environment . . . Earliest and most profound emotional experience . . . Earliest attachments . . . Our emotions raw and uncovered . . . We begin to feel things . . . Attitude of others toward us . . .
7 CHARIOT	Our physical support systems . . . Physical extensions of the self . . . End of Stage Two: Emotional . . . Beginning of Stage Three: Mental
8 STRENGTH	Our emotional support systems . . . The emotional package gets rationalized/systematized . . . Mental side of emotions Status of formalized relationships/marriage . . . Emotional growth . . . We begin to know and understand our feelings . . . Our heart tells us what to do . . .
9 HERMIT	Our philosophy . . . Attitude . . . Approach . . . Our game plan . . . Our rules . . . Our thoughts about our thoughts . . . Caterpillar before the butterfly . . .
10 WHEEL	Spiritual Stage of Spiritual Plane . . . The present moment . . . Major message from God . . . Present super-conscious The awakening . . . The butterfly emerges . . . We have the courage to spin The Wheel of Fortune . . . Turn to faith . . . What we must get on with . . . Major aspect of this reading . . . No way to know until we commit, then we are told . . . End of Stage Three: Mental . . . Beginning of Stage Four: Spiritual

Suit	#	Card	Description
S / W	11	JUSTICE	Conscious mind at the present moment . . . Plans for the future . . . Major decisions appear here . . . Mental decisions . . . Ability to communicate verbally Status of Throat Chakra
C / W	12	HANGED MAN	Present state of emotions . . . Present sub-conscious . . . Innermost desires Decisions of the heart appear here . . . Disposition of Heart Chakra and/or Solar Plexus and/or Genital Chakra
P / S	13	DEATH	Physical situation at present moment . . . The effect of Higher Mind and the love of truth on the body . . . Status of Root/Anal Chakra . . . End of Stage Four: Spiritual . . . Beginning of Stage Five: Higher Mental . . .
C / S	14	TEMPERANCE	Effect of Higher Mind on Emotional near future . . . Higher understanding of Emotional nature . . . Taking Emotional stock . . .
S / S	15	DEVIL	Devil is Mental/Mental position . . . Evil as total mental fabrication by man's conscious level . . . Where our will-to-know and love-of-truth lead us to a confrontation of aspects of evil heretofore unaware of. For complete growth we must have knowledge of evil . . . but not necessarily direct experience of evil. Major potential temptation/detour off our intended path . . . Off our Karmic Contract . . . Status of the ego . . .
W / C	16	TOWER	Flashes of intuition from Higher Mind at the Spiritual Level . . . How we shift from love of truth to love of life . . . How to begin our Higher Emotional Stage . . . Next major input from God . . . End of Stage Five: Higher Mental . . . Beginning of Stage Six: Higher Emotional
S / C	17	STAR	Revelations of right thought . . . Effect of love of life and compassion on thought . . . Effect of our philosophy at work . . . Outcome of temptations of position 15 and input from God, position 16 . . . Ability to communicate feelings . . . Major new ideas . . . Emotional evaluation of our achievements . . .
C / C	18	MOON	Our compassionate nature . . . Our attitude toward others . . . Mid-range future of our Emotional Nature . . . This position is Emotion/Emotion . . .
P / P	19	SUN	Physical harvest . . . Ego begins to melt under heat of sun Disposition for final Stage in life . . . Ultimate evolution of the five senses . . . Long-term physical health . . . Physical legacies (wills) End of Stage Six: Higher Emotional . . . Beginning of Stage Seven: Higher Physical
C / P	20	JUDGEMENT	Emotional harvest . . . Our heart's review of life's performance. Long-term what we will feel the most . . . Care the most about . . . What will rule our hearts . . .
S / P	21	WORLD	Mental harvest . . . Mental review . . . as we begin to see, know and understand the universe and melt into unity again . . . Mental legacies . . . Teachings . . . Creative works
W / P	22	FOOL	The Karmic Contract . . . The "Report Card" on how well we fulfilled our contract

P = Pentacles   C = Cups   S = Swords   W = Wands

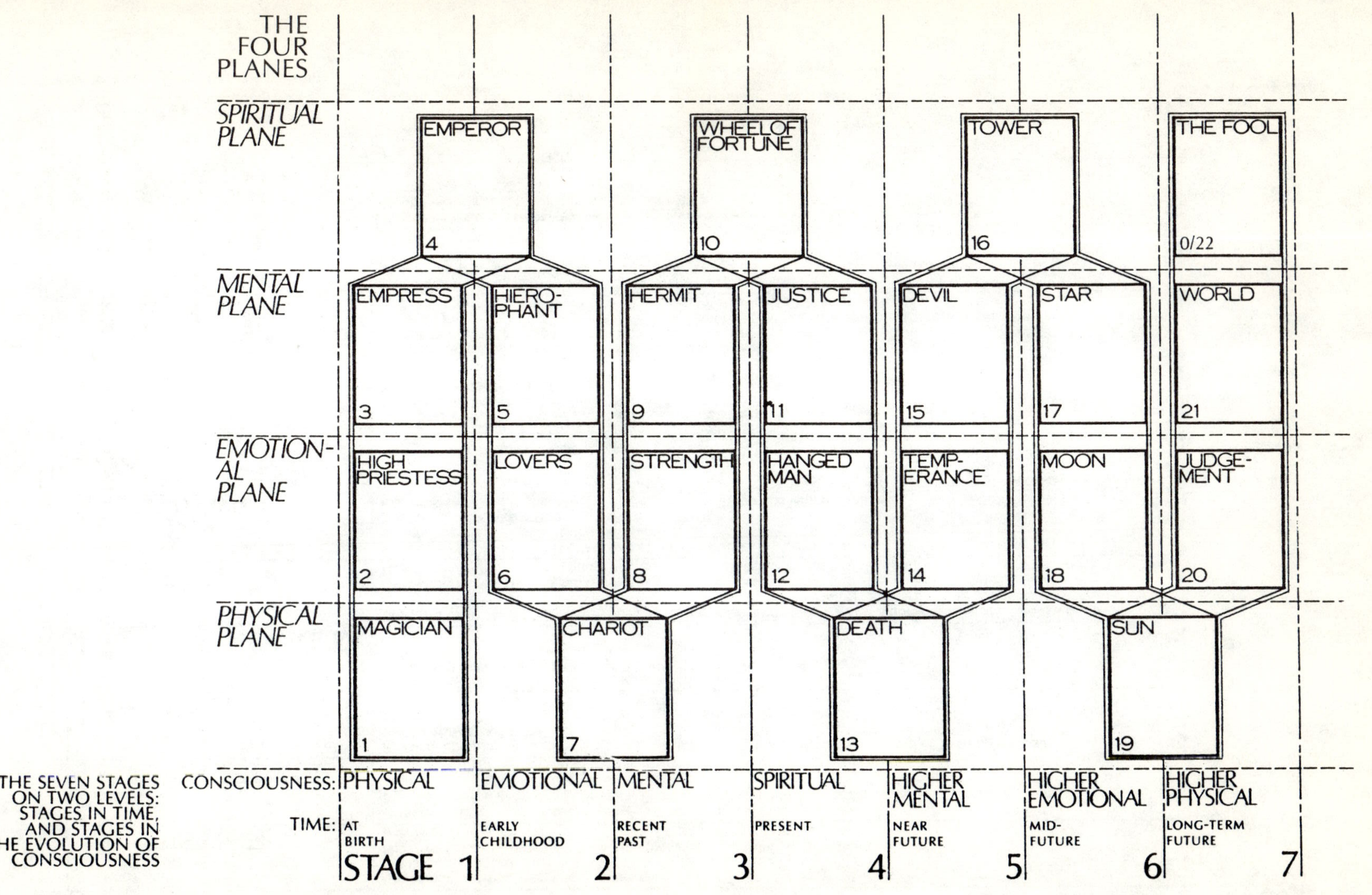

THE FOUR PLANES

SPIRITUAL PLANE
MENTAL PLANE
EMOTION-AL PLANE
PHYSICAL PLANE

EMPEROR 4
WHEEL OF FORTUNE 10
TOWER 16
THE FOOL 0/22

EMPRESS 3
HIERO-PHANT 5
HERMIT 9
JUSTICE 11
DEVIL 15
STAR 17
WORLD 21

HIGH PRIESTESS 2
LOVERS 6
STRENGTH 8
HANGED MAN 12
TEMP-ERANCE 14
MOON 18
JUDGE-MENT 20

MAGICIAN 1
CHARIOT 7
DEATH 13
SUN 19

THE SEVEN STAGES ON TWO LEVELS: STAGES IN TIME, AND STAGES IN THE EVOLUTION OF CONSCIOUSNESS

CONSCIOUSNESS: PHYSICAL EMOTIONAL MENTAL SPIRITUAL HIGHER MENTAL HIGHER EMOTIONAL HIGHER PHYSICAL

TIME: AT BIRTH EARLY CHILDHOOD RECENT PAST PRESENT NEAR FUTURE MID-FUTURE LONG-TERM FUTURE

STAGE 1 2 3 4 5 6 7

respects; that's the trick. Not one or the other, not one for a little time and then the other—both of them at the same time. They exist at apparent extremes, as points at the limits, so that we can conceive of what's in between, what those limits conscribe. The points themselves do not exist except as a mental, abstract concept. What really exists is everything in between. Duality is a function of the mind that is able to define and confine things for us. The practical definition of everything in between is, of course, relative.

Tarot knows and teaches well the illusions and realities of duality and paradox. This is its strong point. There is nothing in the world that deals with duality like Tarot. But especially and most importantly it deals with the duality of good and evil. And more specifically, that of God and the devil. These, too, are abstract points at the extremes of conceptual mental limits. What exists is everything in the middle, and it is all God, all of it.

Tarot proves that evil is only a mental concept. We know that rocks and trees aren't evil. We know that animals aren't evil. We have to get to man before we see evil surface. And man is not evil at the physical level; our bodies are not evil. Man is not evil at the emotional level; our hearts are not evil. We have to get to the level of the mind of man before we can see evil. The structure of the Tarot shows this truth.

Karmic Tarot presents a way of studying the evolution of our consciousness. All the questions we have, all the decisions to be made, the problems to be solved, can be brought to the Karmic Spread because all of our questions relate to our progress on the path, and our path is our evolution of consciousness. We are all waking up at various speeds to the reality of what we really are. Modern physicists finally are now saying and proving what metaphysicians have always known—that everything is energy, or better said, everything is vibration. I believe that the Tarot, both Major and Minor Arcana, was conceived with the knowledge in mind that all is energy. The two Arcana can be seen to be energy patterns. They are literally sine curves visibly pulsing to numerous rhythms that we can study in their symbology. These rhythms give valuable information to the meanings of individual cards, while suggesting a new layout for their interpretation, the Karmic Spread. In addition, the structure of each of the Arcana lends itself to defining the other. The Karmic Spread itself is literally a graphic grid of the inner action of the two Arcana.

The Tarot is a living language. The cards are like the letters in our alphabet, except that they are infinitely richer because they are not flat and meaningless before being combined. The cards as letters of the Tarot alphabet are in a sense three-dimensional, each speaking to us alone and in combination. We should not be confused by the variance of method, meaning or interpretation. Part of the magic of the Tarot is its ability to speak to each reader personally in terms known only to that reader. God knows what a given reader's interpretations of given cards, of given positions in given spreads will be, and He will provide accordingly for the "dialect" of that reader. Another reader might be given other cards, in other positions and in other spreads. In the living language of Tarot there are as many dialects as there are readers.

RACHEL POLLACK

An Overview of the Variety of New Tarot Decks: Emphasis on European Decks

THE IDEA FOR MY FORTHCOMING BOOK ON CONtemporary Tarot decks (*The New Tarot*) originated because I had collected a few Tarot decks and I kept seeing more and more decks that I liked very much. I saw so many different and wonderful decks that I knew I could never afford to buy them all. So I thought to myself, How could I acquire these decks for free? And I realized I could write a book about all the different decks and I'd get review copies. So this basically worked.

To a slight extent the decks that I have featured in my book are the ones that publishers gave me. And I was very lucky in that Stuart Kaplan of U.S. Games Systems, Inc., gave me many review decks. This was very generous of him. So that is how I became a collector.

I also met a lot of nice people. I renewed my acquaintances with Billy Potts, who did the new Amazon Tarot, and I also got to meet Susan Wheat, who had been involved with the Amazon Tarot and had then gone on to create her own decks.

In the course of working on all this, I was studying the question of what is happening with all these different decks. Why do we have so many? Does anything tie them together? Why, suddenly, is this going on—this Tarot renaissance? Is it simply that it is the time for Tarot, or is there something deeper? What is causing this tremendous freedom, this tremendous surge of creativity in designing decks? And I came up with the idea that people are doing what I call "reimagining" the Tarot. They are delving into tradition and coming up with something new—and not being afraid to experiment. People are giving themselves the freedom to create new Tarots, things that have not been seen before. Tarots that go in new artistic directions, or Tarots that link to other cultures, or Tarots that move away from symbols and into storytelling. So, the movement I call reimagining is the idea that people are inspired by the traditional concepts but don't feel bound to them. People feel that the time has come to create a whole range of Tarots. Previously the impulse was to find the one true Tarot—"The Tarot," and people would argue about which was the true one. There was a situation with the Golden Dawn Qabalist System, and the Eliphas Levi Qabalist System: Because they were different, the Golden Dawn people claimed that Eliphas Levi knew his system was wrong and deliberately put it forth that way to confuse people so they wouldn't learn the truth. So there have been these kind of arguments.

Now people are saying that it doesn't have to be this way. We can say that the Tarot is a fluid kind of archetype rather than a fixed archetype, and therefore all these things are true. The Fool is the first card; it's also the last, and also the next to the last. Justice is number eight, and it's also number eleven, and it's possible to mingle them, and it's possible to keep your mind open and look at both things at once rather than being fixated on only one. And once we make that jump, it becomes possible to see that we can do all kinds of new things that haven't been done before.

A lot of people, when they see some of the new decks that are so different, think they're nice and very pretty, but they're not Tarot. Usually what these people mean, when you get down to it, is that it's not the first deck they were familiar with, the Rider-Waite-Smith deck. But the Rider deck itself is a late development, published in 1910, and it includes many things that had never been seen before then, things that some other people have soundly rejected. So, that position doesn't hold at all. And then there are people who feel that The Marseilles is the true Tarot—the classic one—or at least that form is the true form, where, for example, the Juggler is card number one, the Fool has the dog or the cat biting it, and the Lovers has the young man standing between a dark and a light woman

Le Tarot de Marseille

with a cupid overhead. The female Pope sits there with a hat, and she has a book in her lap, or sometimes a scroll. So some people say this is the classic Tarot, this is the true Tarot form. But when we look back, we discover that it actually is not, because these depictions arose later than the first deck. These are classic forms, but they are not as old as fifteenth-century decks, such as the Visconti-Bembo. So the one people say you can't change because it's the true official, genuine Tarot, isn't.

The point is that the Tarot has always been fluid. It's always changed a lot. One of the theories of the Tarot is that it represented the various Renaissance virtues and social situations. There you see the four virtues, one of which is strength, traditionally pictured as Hercules killing the lion. The Wheel of Fortune and Death are moral lessons. They are lessons in democracy to a large extent, but they could also be traced back to shamanist and Goddess concepts. The Wheel of Fortune could be traced back to the Goddess Fortuna. Death could be traced back to the shamanist encounter with the skeleton as a personal experience. In Christian times that became a moral lesson: kings and queens and the powerful had to die like anybody else. We see Death harvesting the crowned heads of Europe in most of the traditional cards. So, when we look at the Tarot we find that nothing is really fixed. Nothing can be said to be original and true. What we *can* say is mostly true is the idea of seventy-eight cards, because, from what knowledge we have, that does go back all the way to the fifteenth century.

There is also one card that to my knowledge is found fairly unchanged from the very earliest cards. Even in most of the modern decks, where almost everything else has been changed to something completely different, this card somehow always manages to stay the same. It is the Hanged Man, or the Hanged One in the decks where it is a woman. But it's almost always the same kind of picture—somebody hanging upside down, usually by one foot, though sometimes with both feet bound. This card has varied the least throughout the centuries. In a new deck called the Haindl deck, which I'll discuss in more detail later, you'll see that for the most part the Major Arcana pictures bear no resemblance to the traditional ones. The themes are the same, the concepts are built upon the traditional ones, but the pictures are completely different. Yet when the artist, Herman Haindl, was creating these cards, he found himself depicting the Hanged Man in the same traditional way, with his own concept of it added on. The Hanged Man has a fascinating quality of hypnotizing people. This is why the Hanged Man seems to me to embody the essence of the esoteric Tarot, because it has this powerful image people can't get away from, that they don't want to change. They want to keep that one picture the way they've seen it before.

Another new deck just coming out is called the Merlin Tarot. It was designed by Robert Stewart, who has written books on Merlin and King Arthur and Celtic tradition, and it was painted by Miranda Gray. It's based not only on Arthurian legend but also on an older, or simultaneous, tradition of Merlin as a Welsh magician. The particular works that Stewart referred to were the *Vita Merlini*, the *Life of Merlin* by Geoffrey of Monmouth, and the *Prophesies of Merlin*. Stewart has written books about both of these works, and they're well worth reading. His deck design incorporates the universal view, the esoteric system of Celtic initiation and tradition, as symbolized in these stories and prophesies of Merlin.

In his analysis of the *Vita Merlini* he gives you the plot, with quotations from the poem. Then he shows you how the underlying symbolism is based on the tradition of the land, of the Celtic pagan closeness to the Earth. He looks at images in the *Vita Merlini* that pertain to the Tarot to demonstrate that the symbolic scenes and people and encounters are the same ones found in the Major Arcana. If true, this would be very significant, since the *Vita Merlini* was written a few hundred years before the first Tarot deck that we know of appeared. Therefore this shows a kind of ongoing tradition that had its expression in Celtic lands.

Some of the connections that Stewart makes are a little bit tenuous, because if you're going to discuss spirituality, you're bound to have images such as a powerful king for an Emperor, or a Queen who is part of nature for an Empress, and so on. But there is one aspect that's really fascinating, and that is the story that Stewart retells in his book. He calls the story "The Threefold Death." He says, and he's probably right about this, that this story comes down to us as an entertaining tale, but it's actually what anthropologists call a screening story for a ritual. That is, it's a light folktale that actually derives from secret initiation ceremonies in the Celtic mysteries.

The story is that Merlin comes to court. He's been in the woods living the life of a mad hermit, but he recovers his sanity through the help of magic and comes to court. At the court are the king and queen; she is Merlin's sister. Merlin looks at them and bursts out laughing. The king asks why he is laughing, and Merlin says because your wife, my sister, is cuckolding you. She's having an affair with that other guy over there. And the king is furious at being humiliated this way. Stewart points out that there is no hint in the poem of this being evil on the queen's part; it's really more of an embarrassment, something that's funny. The king doesn't like being made fun of, and the queen has to think fast because she's in trouble. So she says to her husband, "How can you believe my brother? He's a madman. He's a prophet. He's a nut. How can you believe him? Look, I'll prove it to you."

She brings up a young boy from the court and says to Merlin, "How will this boy die?"

And Merlin says, "He will die by a fall from a high place."

So she takes the boy out, cuts his hair, puts different clothes on him, brings him back in and says to Merlin, "How will this boy die?"

And Merlin says, "He will be hanged from a tree." And people in the court start to snicker. Then she takes the boy out and disguises him as a girl, and brings him back in and says to merlin, "And how will this one die?"

And Merlin says, "Girl or not, this one will die by drowning." So now the whole court is in an uproar, and the king feels his wife is vindicated because this prophet can't even tell the difference between the same person in three different suits of clothes.

The story then tells how later on in life, years later, the boy grows up and goes hunting with his dogs, and he gets wildly excited chasing a deer.

The deer, the hart as it was called, was the symbol in medieval poetry of the mystic quest. He is chasing this hart, this mystic quest, and he doesn't realize he's come to a cliff. Spurred on by his dogs, he falls off the cliff. So, first we have the Fool, falling off the cliff in the mystic quest. And then when he falls, his foot catches in a tree. With his foot caught in a tree, his head ends up in the river and he drowns. So, the image we have now is the Hanged Man, because he's hanging by one foot from a tree with his head in water. Most Hanged Man cards do not have water in the picture. But in some of the esoteric decks, such as the Golden Dawn, water was added. It is seen as the key, and the key is the dissolution, the dissolving of ego. This is the point of the Hanged Man. And this is why it's upside down, because it represents a release from the ego, a release from that which usually fixes us in our rigid positions.

So this poem, written long before the first Tarot we know of, provides a clear description of the Hanged Man as a symbolic initiation on three different levels, and also of the Fool, including the dogs. It's mysterious that this image draws us backward to the question of origins and also takes us into the present, where we find this story in the Merlin Tarot. In that deck, the Fool is shown hunting with his dogs, standing with them on the cliff before the fall. And then the Hanged Man is shown with his foot in the tree. This also shows the concept that *before* the fall is the Fool: the Fool is innocent. This is something that many of us have come to through contemplating the Fool in, say, the Rider or Golden Dawn decks or some of the modern Tarots. And we have the same concept, the same connection between the Fool and the falling, in the *Vita Merlini*.

In looking at and working on all these different Tarots, I wanted to see how all these things fit together. I tend to take an organizing approach to things. I considered the many different themes and I came up with seven main ones. There are decks that are primarily for art, decks that are popular, decks that are what I call storytelling decks, and decks I've labeled cultural, feminist, psychological, and esoteric. It's interesting to see what people are doing in each of these areas.

The esoteric Tarots are probably closest to the ones we think of as traditional. Nicholas Tereshchenko's deck and Eileen Connolly's deck are two that I would describe as fitting into that category. These decks work with symbolic structures, with Qabalistic tradition, with very precise symbols, the vocabulary of symbols—they are very much of a tradition in

6 THE LOVERS

9 THE HERMIT

The Golden Dawn Tarot

which we recognize things. The Tereshchenko deck has the Golden Dawn symbolism worked into it and written along the sides. The Connolly deck also uses a great deal of that same symbolism we find in the Golden Dawn, Rider, or BOTA decks, and so on.

One of the important developments in this field was the publication of the Golden Dawn Tarot in the 1970s. This was a major event because it was the first time that the deck used within the Golden Dawn was revealed to the public. It was presented by Robert Wang, who also wrote a couple of books about it. According to Wang, he followed the tradition of copying the original deck that was revealed to McGregor Mathers and painted by his wife Fiona. Every initiate, every person who joined the Golden Dawn, was expected to copy this deck by painting it themselves as closely as possible. Wang copied the late Israel Regardie's copy. Then he made some changes that brought it closer to the text which described Mathers's original deck. That's really the essence of the esoteric concept—that you copy precisely a revealed deck, a deck that has come from spiritual channeling, and this deck at the same time contains precise symbols. So you have a double-sided truth: one side is not to be changed because it's absolute truth, coming from the angels, and the other side is in a symbolic structured form.

Another deck that's very interesting is the Tree of Life Tarot, designed by Rufus Camphausen and drawn by Appalonia van Leeuwen. This deck simply shows the Tree of Life, the famous structure of the ten

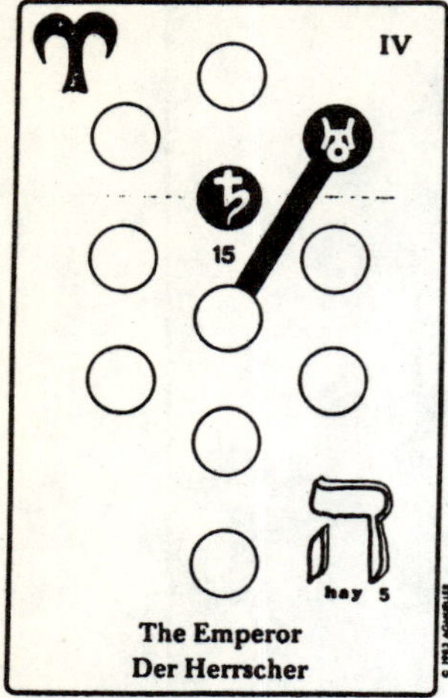

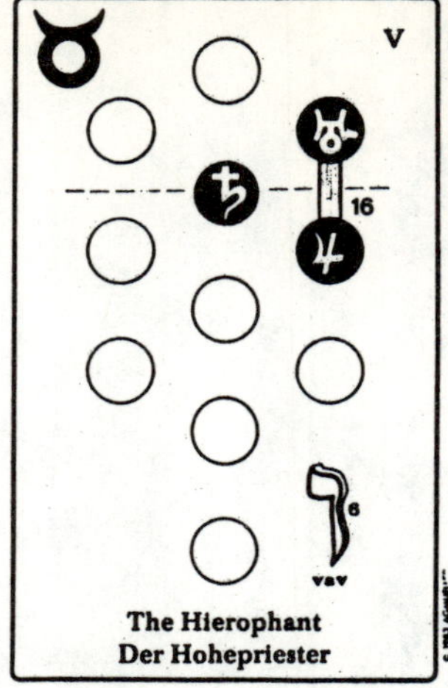

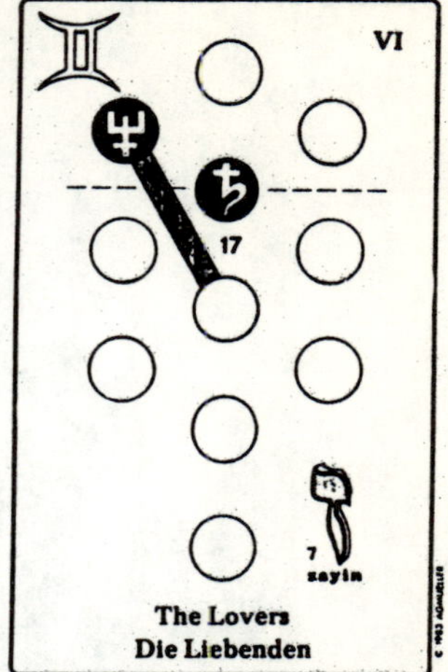

The Tree of Life Tarot

Sephiroth with the twenty-two lines connecting them. On each of the Major cards we find the line. As you know, each Major card has a line connecting it to the ten Sephiroth, and that line is illuminated, with the Tree all in black. It's all dark and one line will be illuminated: that line will be the card it represents. For each of the four suits you have whichever Sephira represents it illuminated; one of the ten circles is brightly colored, and the four suits each have a different key color for their element. So let's say, from one to ten, the Ace is Kether, the crown chakra, the Crown Sephirah. And therefore, for the Suit of Cups, in which the color is blue for water, the top circle would be colored blue and the other circles would be dark. The court cards use the four-letter name of God, Yod Heh Vav Heh, and again, the color for the particular suit. So instead of one letter being illuminated, it progresses from the King on down. The King is illuminated first—the King is Yod, fire—and so on, ending up with the Princess, in which all four letters are brightly colored. The Minor Arcana progresses from having just one Sephirah colored, then two, then three, until finally the ten of the suit has all ten illuminated. You can use these for study, as kinds of flash cards. If you're memorizing which pathway is the Fool, you can look at that card and see which path is lighted on the Tree. You can also use these cards to see a kind of graphic demonstration of how the Tree progresses into life, into creation. It can be a very powerful image as you set them in order and see that color moving down the Tree to the bottom so that it becomes more and more vibrant with energy.

There is an interesting French deck called the Masonic Tower, which uses symbolism from Freemasonry. This is a very dense deck, with cards that can be difficult to look at sometimes because the drawing style is very crude. The main impact comes from this very dense imagery of the Freemasonry tradition. If you don't know that tradition you can easily get lost and not really catch everything that's there. But if you do know it, or if you want to study it, this deck becomes a wonderful tool to do that.

There are several astrological decks. The Mandala Astrological Tarot is a Tarot that uses abstract symbols of the planets and signs and elements on the cards, rather than people. This deck gives you a clear sense of the connections between the Tarot and the different levels of astrological symbols. In fact, that deck really uses the Golden Dawn system. One of the great contributions the Golden Dawn made was in formulating a complete system in which each card was linked to something in astrology. Most decks since then have generally followed this method, although various ones changed certain details.

There is also a deck called The Astro Tarot by Carol Abrams, which is privately produced. It has very lush, somewhat psychedelic paintings that are meant to illustrate the different astrological qualities of, say, the planets and signs. One of the interesting things Carol does is that she has cards for transits and aspects. For example, she'll have a trine card or a conjunction card, and match them up to the planets and signs in a very special way. It's a photographic deck. To create each new deck, she makes prints from her negatives, then mounts them on cardboard and laminates them. The deck is available by mail order.

So these are some of the things people are doing in the esoteric tradition. Another thing that's very interesting now is the idea of actual new cards.

For example, Nicholas Tereshchenko speaks in his work about discoveries of new Arcana, going beyond the accepted twenty-two. This ties in with work by Timothy Leary and Robert Anton Wilson, in which they suggest that there are twenty-four rather than twenty-two Major Arcana. We now find some decks that reflect this. One of them is called Kirwan Cards, which is just being published. They are also called Matrix Cards. They are interesting for two reasons: first, because there are two new cards, called double zero and triple zero, which makes me think of a roulette table. These are then used to form a Kabbalistic triad. As you know, in the Kabbalistic system there are three levels, called Ain, Ain Soph, and Ain Soph Aur. They are like three levels of nothingness, or like three

Harris-Crowley Thoth Tarot

levels of infinity in mathematics. Kirwan has used this idea and created these two extra cards to fit these different levels. The other thing that's interesting about Kirwan's cards is that he's taking esoteric ideas and bringing them out for a general audience. For example, instead of having the Tarot forms for his court cards, he uses Jack, Queen, and King, like a playing deck; he calls the fourth one the Mistress. He depicts people in ordinary modern life, not in medieval times. He's created designs that people outside our esoteric New Age spiritual world can easily grasp, and at the same time, he uses the esoteric Tarot principles.

Similarly, by a nice synchronicity, the new edition of the Lady Frieda Harris-Aleister Crowley deck also has two extra cards—two other versions of the Magus, the Magician—which can be used as well to symbolize these other levels of zero, double zero, and triple zero.

Another theme is that of the art decks. By this I mean decks in which the main focus is in using the Tarot as an art form to create something of beauty, something that will stir people by the wonder of its images. There is one deck called The Picini Tarot, by an Italian artist. The pictures are very abstract, and the descriptions are completely lost in a kind of wild, obscure symbolism. The artist had as his primary focus creating something that expresses his artistic style.

Another one that probably you have seen is the Dali Tarot. This deck by Salvador Dali, possibly with the help of others, has been the subject of

Niki de St. Phalle Tarot

a controversy over authorship. Amanda Lear claims that she created most of it. Others claim that's not true, that Lear simply wants publicity. In any case, this deck takes Dali's personal surrealist vocabulary of symbols, marries them to the history of art, and then manages to fit the images perfectly to the Rider deck. For example, in the Minor Arcana there is a picture taken from eighteenth-century French art which looks like one of Pamela Smith's drawings. He's done this matching up very well. Everything comments on everything else, so there are Dali's surrealist crutches, melting watches, and so on, commenting on classical forms from traditional European paintings. And at the same time, both of these styles derive extra meaning from their connection to the Tarot tradition.

The Niki de St. Phalle Tarot statues in Italy are a truly wonderful development in the world of Tarot. Niki de St. Phalle is a well-known sculptress who creates colorful, monumental works. Currently, she is building a set of twenty-two statues, actually about twenty, because a couple are being combined. It's her greatest work up to now, she says. They are on a hill in Tuscany, near Capalvio. Some of the statues are as tall as four stories! When you drive up the road you see them above the trees, and they gleam with light. Niki first designs a metal frame, then pours concrete into it to make the building, and finally covers it with mirrors and ceramic tiles in incredibly bright colors. It ends up gleaming in the sun, which bounces off it in all directions.

The Tower is four stories high. It's a very simple form, a tower building with the top sort of blown off, and a machine in the middle. The machine was done by Jean Tingueley, her husband and partner. They are no longer together as husband and wife but they work together often. When it is finished, the machine will revolve. As you probably know, Tingueley's art is full of cranks and wheels and pulleys. When you push a button or step on something, everything starts going around and making noise, often a deliberate creaking noise, so it sounds old and rusty. The Tower is completely covered with mirrors so that at night, especially if there are a full moon and stars, it's really a magnificent sight. The Tarot Garden has been featured in several major magazines, even though it's not finished yet.

The artist herself is living inside the statue of the Empress, which is the Sphinx, while she's completing the project. It's a beautiful, airy building. Her bedroom is in the shoulder of the Sphinx. When she's finished, she's probably going to make that building a writer's retreat. Every now and then some lucky writer will get to live for a while in the Empress while completing a project.

Another of the seven themes is the area I call the "cultural Tarots." One of these decks is the Xultun Tarot of the Mayan Indians, by Peter Balin. This deck was one of the very first which dared to link the Tarot with something that essentially has nothing to do with Tarot. Peter Balin's work is a statement of how the Tarot and other traditions are linked to the same ancient discoveries of the human race.

Subsequent decks followed this example. Some are done completely in another tradition, the most well known of which is probably the Native American deck, beautifully drawn and very detailed in its ideas. Some people don't care for this because it seem too sociological. They think it's interesting to see how Native Americans prepared for the winter by storing fruit, for example, but this doesn't help them much in their own reading and meditation. This is more often true outside America. In the United States, people are more drawn to this deck.

Other kinds of cultural Tarots are various new Egyptian decks. Previously people claimed that the Tarot was Egyptian in origin and used Egyptian imagery. The Thoth deck by Crowley and Harris has some Egyptian imagery, the Church of Light is very Egyptian, and so are some of the earlier French decks. But these were really more esoteric than cultural. They were European and American peoples' esoteric concepts of Egyptian mythology and symbolism, coming from Madame Blavatsky rather than from Egypt. Now there are some new decks, such as the Tarot of Transition and Egipcios Kier's cards, which actually depict Egyptian culture. Egipcios Kier shows daily life in ancient Egypt, and links this to themes in the Tarot. It works as a Tarot deck and also for giving you the religious beliefs, practices, social set-up, and so on, of ancient Egypt.

The Tarot of Transition deck is fascinating because you can use it as a new way of reading. It presents the Major Arcana as the Gods and Goddesses of Egypt, but it gives a different order for them and creates its own mythology. That mythology is the judgment of the soul after death in the Egyptian afterworld, the land of the dead. When you approach these cards through a reading, you're asking that your soul be judged, and they give you favorable and unfavorable omens. It's a very intriguing system, worth looking into.

Another interesting cultural-type deck is the Kashmir Tarot. This is a deck by a Dutchman named Nico van de Beek. He calls it the Kashmir Tarot because it was begun in Kashmir, when Nico and his wife, Ann Rehder, were traveling and living in India for a while and were involved with Tibetan people in Nepal. He conceived of making a deck, and since he wanted it to be a woodcut deck, he traveled to Kashmir, where they have master woodcutters. He found an artisan who made him a prototype deck carved out of walnut. It was begun on the full moon of Shiva's birthday and finished on the full moon of the Buddha's birthday. These cards are relief carvings on thick wood, really solid. They come in a wooden box and cost around two thousand dollars a copy.

Knowing that not too many people would want to spend two thousand dollars for their next deck, Nico decided to do a regular card version as well. But he wanted this also to have a special quality. So instead of drawing the cards or painting them and then having them photographed and printed with the usual four-color process, he had them silk-screened. He went through a hundred thousand silk-screens to get the different colors, so it's really a magnificent deck. And they link the Tarot to Tibetan Buddhism. So along with the Tarot symbolism there is some very beautiful imagery: for example, the Hermit shown in the Himalayan mountains.

The development of women's Tarots has become known through the Motherpeace deck and Daughters of the Moon. There is a new Amazon Tarot which is worth tracking down. The main feature of this deck is that it was done by a collective of some twenty-three artists. One reason they

Kasmir Tarot

did this as a collective was that they didn't want it to be simply one person's vision. They wanted the design to be created by many people, so they put out the word that they were looking for images for the Tarot. They received many wonderful pictures. Sometimes they received two for the same card, and they used both. There were two versions of card fourteen, which they called Art; two versions of the Lovers, and so on. The deck uses many different artistic styles. It has pen and ink, papercuts, and photographs. It's a wonderful project.

Women's decks are being designed not simply to bring Tarot principles together with the women's movement. The goal, which is very radical, is to go beyond that. It's to create a new culture, to completely transform human culture and human relationships into the divine, through images. These decks are reimagined because they wish to liberate the Tarot from an imagery that is seen as patriarchal.

Another interesting deck is the Barbara Walker deck, which is somewhat unusual. Its main purpose is to provide knowledge of the history of Goddesses and Goddess-centered religion. It complements her two books, *Secrets of the Tarot* and *The Woman's Encyclopedia of Myths and Secrets.* Barbara Walker is a researcher who has collected incredible masses of information, which she links together in her works. Sometimes the information is questionable. If you know something about a subject, you wonder where she got certain information. But her work is a great pleasure to

Daughters of the Moon Tarot

read, because you feel almost lost in a whole continent of facts that she displays and links together in wonderful ways.

The psychological theme encompasses a group of Tarots which seem to focus on reaching essential psychological states. Their aim is to transform people through finding images that will perfectly capture conditions of mind, of being, conditions of relationships between people, people's hopes, fears, desires, and so on. Very often these are modern images. I think of the Voyager Tarot as the supreme example of this kind of deck, in that it uses the Tarot tradition and follows the ancient esoteric concepts, yet it's also very modern. It's oriented toward finding the essences of people's beings and thereby leading them to transform that being.

Another of the psychological decks is one called the Philosopher's Stone, which actually is not a Tarot at all. This is a playful thing in which all the pictures are of stone heads, like those on Easter Island, presented in different formulations to bring up psychological issues. For example, one of them shows two stone heads that are trying to come together but there is a little stone between them. Their foreheads are both touching it, so they push as hard as they can but they can't get through that block to touch or join with each other. The next picture shows that they have each turned their heads to the side, so that they are now resting against each other, and the little stone has fallen away. They're looking in different directions but their heads are touching. These are very graphic demonstrations of the ways people relate and communicate with each other.

Der Herrscher

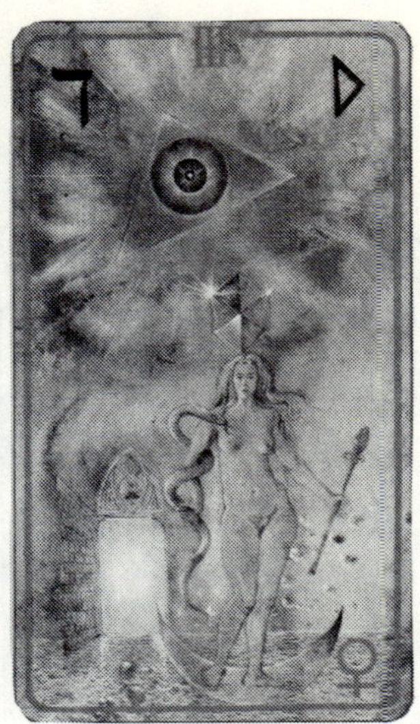

Die Herrscherin

Haindl Tarot

I mentioned earlier a new deck called the Haindl Tarot, by the German artist Herman Haindl. I've just completed book to go with that deck. So far the book is available only in German. I'm aiming for an English version as well, and to have an American edition of the deck. In the Haindl Tarot, the Major Arcanas were done in a very special way. The artist allowed himself to get an idea of what he wanted to say and what kind of qualities he wanted, and then opened himself up to whatever came. So the pictures were done spontaneously, in a kind of channeling. At the same time Herman, who is sixty years old and has spent a lifetime painting, can automatically structure paintings and create compositions. So these are beautiful paintings and are very organized despite the fact that they were done without conscious planning of what symbols he would use. The cards create their own kind of myth, in which the patriarchal society has left its roots in the Earth. This has led to an ecological crisis and to the destruction of the Earth and the dishonoring of the feminine.

In the Haindl deck the card that is given in some sense the most power is the Empress. The Empress shows a naked woman rising out of the sea and standing on a lunar crescent while a triangle with an eye in it gleams with light above her head. Also touching her is a six-sided crystal. The deck uses Runes as well as Hebrew letters. The Empress represents the true creative power of the Goddess.

The next card is the Emperor, a young, very dynamic figure, meant to be Odin and representing the young gods and young patriarchal religions.

These have not only taken over from the ancient matriarchal religions but have banished all memory of them, which is why we are told in school that the world began some five thousand years ago. If we are not told this by some creationists, our histories always begin with ancient Egypt, several thousand years ago, giving the impression that nothing existed before then. In fact, before that was the period when the patriarchal takeover occurred. And so we see Odin striding away from the big tree behind him—the world tree that is also the Earth, the mother—and he's denying that existence. Then the story progresses, showing different aspects, but when it gets to the Hanged Man we see something wonderful. The Hanged Man is shown hanging from a tree, his leg is tied, and there is a Venus symbol in the tree, the symbol of the Goddess. It's silver, the same color as the moon. He hangs down with his hands out, instead of behind his back, in a kind of joy—an openness to surrender. He is surrendering to the Earth: as his hair hangs down, it becomes rooted to the ground.

So these are some of the kinds of modern Tarot decks that people have been working with, and some of the interesting, new, and exciting directions in which Tarot is taking them.

XXIIII
23
THE ALL-POWERFUL GREAT FIRE DRAGON
THE DROWNED SLEEPING TITAN
IIIII
55

NICOLAS TERESHCHENKO

Arcanum XXIII: The Drowned Sleeping Titan

> Rejoice with me; for I have found my sheep which was lost . . . Rejoice with me; for I have found the piece which I had lost . . . For this my son was dead, and is alive again; he was lost, and is found . . . be glad: for this thy brother was dead, and is alive again; and was lost, and is found.
>
> —Luke 15:6, 9, 24, 32

THERE IS A LITTLE-KNOWN RABBINICO-TAL-mudic and Qabalistic tradition that, at the time of Creation, the Divine Alphabet had 23 letters,[1] and that the number of books of the Torah was seven, so that it was a Heptateuch and not a Pentateuch as it is now.[2] But one of these letters became invisible[3] when Adam failed to wake up fully from the "deep sleep" which "the Lord caused to fall upon Adam" (Genesis 2:21), for the purpose well known to us all.[4] This suggests that the Major Arcana of the Tarot also should be *at least* 23 in number.

Even before learning of this tradition, I had already asked myself, How many Tarot Arcana should there *really* be?

In my book, *The Cosmos Tarot*, published in France, I describe my "Cosmos Tarot" deck, which contains an Arcanum XXII called The Ape of Thoth. I had noticed that one of the Arcana, the Fool (zero), would not stay single. It seemed to divide itself into two, so I named the zero half Furca the Fool, and the other half XXII—The Ape of Thoth. These two are almost mirror images of each other.

I had previously answered in a provisional manner the question of how many Major Arcana there should be in an article in *The Lamp of Thoth*:

In the traditional Tarot pack there are 22 Major and 56 Minor Arcana, the latter being subdivided into four suits of 14 cards each. Each suit is said to correspond to one of the four Elements and is itself further subdivided into two parts: a set of ten numbered cards and a set of four honor, court, or picture cards, called Knight, Queen, King, and Page. There are thus 16 such cards in all (perhaps corresponding to the 16 Geomantic figures?).

As the Tarot cards are thought to be directly related to the Hebrew alphabet and to the Qabalistic Tree of Life, the above numbers appear to be as they are because there are 22 letters in the Hebrew alphabet and 22 Paths in the Tree of Life, in addition to the ten Sephiroth, which are partitioned into four "worlds," each of which corresponds to one of the letters of the Tetragrammaton, YOD-HEY-VAV-HEY.

At least such is the theory, and the existing decks are printed in accordance with it. But are all these points really true? Let us look at each of the items enumerated above more critically.

First of all, are there only 22 letters in the Hebrew alphabet and are all of them consonants? I think not, as five of the letters have two forms—one "normal" form, used when the letter begins a word or is in the body of the word, and another "final" form, used only when it happens to be the last letter of a word. Note that the normal and final forms do *not* have the same numerical value, or measure, so important in Gematria.

Therefore I think there are in fact not 22, but *27* Hebrew letters.[5] Then we have the fact that seven of these letters are called "double" because they each represent *two* different sounds, such as Beth and Pey. And since Pey is one of the letters which has a final as well as the normal form, it seems clear that we are dealing with not just *one* letter, but with *four*. The letter Kaf is another such letter. So on this basis we have to admit that the Hebrew alphabet is made up of 22 basic letters, seven of which are doubles (with two of these having a final form also) and five finals. When added together, this gives us $22+7+2+5=36$ letters altogether!

Is this not an indication that there ought to be at least 36 and not merely 22 Major Arcana, if their Qabalistic origin, or at least relationship, is admitted?

Let us now examine the fact that there are, after all, *vowels* in the

Hebrew language.[6] True, a written form was given to them much later than the so-called consonants (and what sort of "consonants" are Alef, Yod, and Ayin?). But they exist, even if they have the appearance of dots and dashes (called "Masoretic") variously grouped and placed in or under or over the "consonants." There are seven such groups, though there are 14 names for them, according to Gesenius' Hebrew Grammar, indicating 14 sounds. So, if we add these 14 to the 36, we get 50—the number of Jubilee and of the 50 Qabalistic "Gates".[7] Are we to conclude that there should be in fact 50 Major Arcana, and that Mantegna was therefore right after all in having this number of Trumps in his deck?

If this is so, then what about the 22 "paths" between the Sephiroth? But once again, let us be critical: Are there only 22 paths? Try it for yourself. Even with only the ten explicit Sephiroth there are in fact 38 possible connections. And if we admit the existence of Daath as a Sephirah, then there are 50 possible different paths! Perhaps 28 of them are paths of *un*wisdom rather than wisdom, but is this not very consistent with human nature?[8] And, strangely enough, we end again with 50, just as before. Coincidence?[9]

But let us not be too ambitious at present. Let us content ourselves now with adding just one more Key to the Tarot Arcana. This one is named XXIII—The Drowned Sleeping Titan.

From the available fragmentary and mostly indirect indications in more or less veiled words and images, this newly restored Key can be described as follows:

At the bottom of the Great Ocean-Sea, seen as if through a telescope whose lens is surrounded by the Zodiac, lies a naked Giant, his back supported by a rock on which we can distinguish twelve letters of the "Enochian" or Angelic Alphabet in a square.

On the back surface of this rock, which we cannot see except with our Third Eye, is another engraving, showing a Lightning Flash descending and Nahash, the Serpent of Wisdom, ascending, thus indicating the Way of Return, up the Tree of Life.

The Titan's eyes are closed and he is certainly asleep, if not actually dead. His arms and legs are so disposed that at first sight he seems to have taken the shape of a Fylfot Cross, a deosil swastika. His horizontal trunk supports a cube on which we can see Dr. John Dee's Enochian Tablet of Union, but with an additional line, firmly held down by the Titan's right hand.

On the opposite face of the cube, also invisible to us except through a

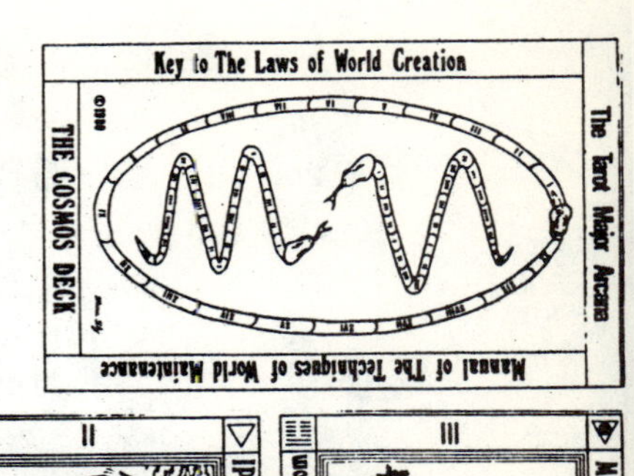

Furca The Fool — The Spirit of Ether

The Juggler — Magician — The Magus of Power

The High Priestess — The Priestess of The Silver Star

The Empress — The Daughter of The Mighty Ones

The Emperor — Son of the Morning, Chief Among the Mighty

The Hierophant — The Magus of The Eternal Gods

The Lover — The Children of The Voice Divine, The Oracle of The Mighty Gods

The Chariot — The Child of The Powers of the Waters, The Lord of The Triumph of Light

Justice

The Hermit

The Turning Wheel

Strength

The Hanged Man

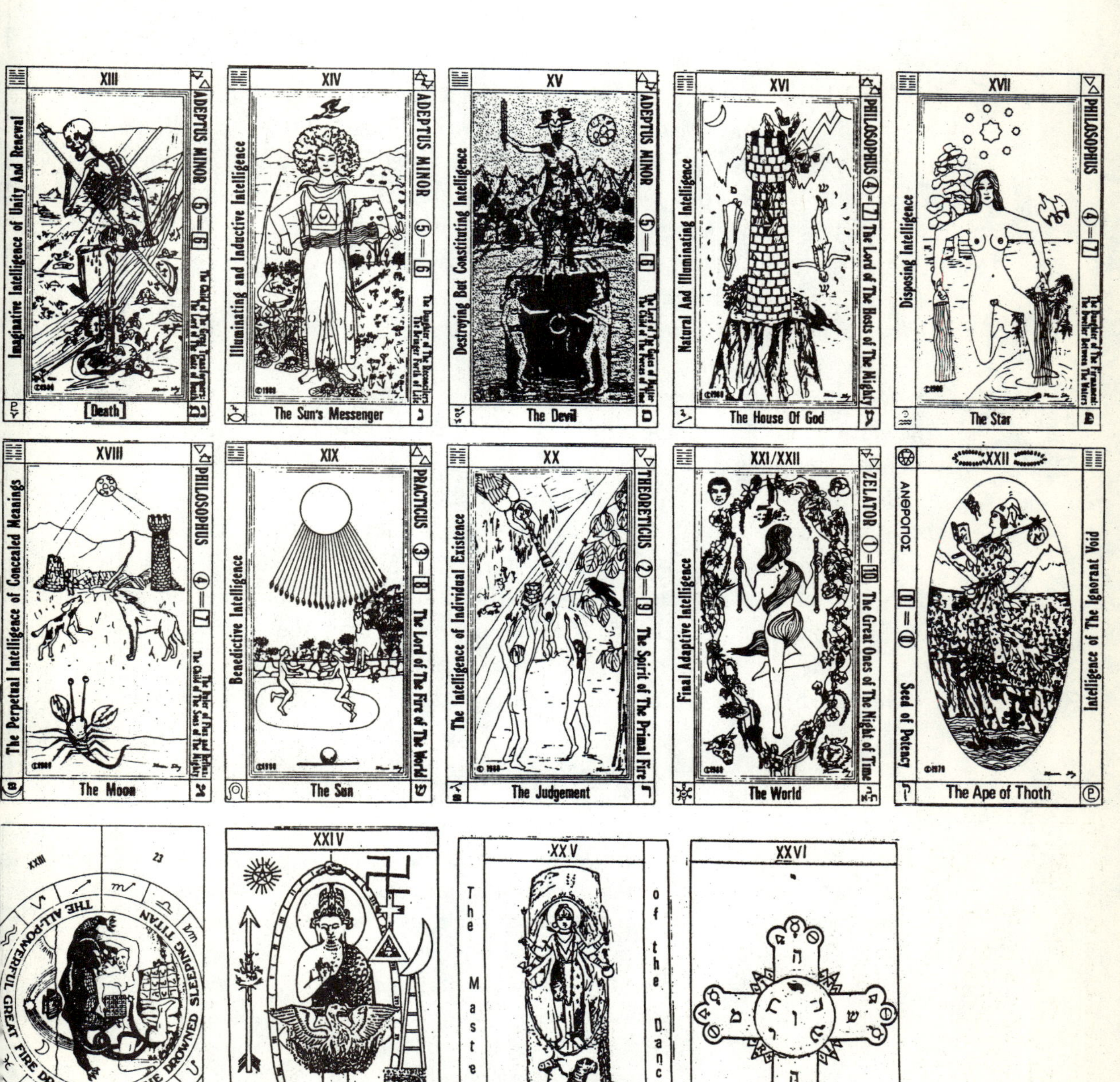

XIII — ADEPTUS MINOR — Imaginative Intelligence of Unity And Renewal — [Death]
XIV — ADEPTUS MINOR — Illuminating and Inductive Intelligence — The Sun's Messenger
XV — ADEPTUS MINOR — Destroying But Constituting Intelligence — The Devil
XVI — PHILOSOPHUS — Natural And Illuminating Intelligence — The House Of God
XVII — PHILOSOPHUS — Disposing Intelligence — The Star
XVIII — PHILOSOPHUS — The Perpetual Intelligence of Concealed Meanings — The Moon
XIX — PRACTICUS — Benedictive Intelligence — The Sun
XX — THEORETICUS — The Intelligence of Individual Existence — The Judgement
XXI/XXII — ZELATOR — Final Adaptive Intelligence — The World
XXII — ANΘΡΟΠΟΣ — Seed of Potency — Intelligence of The Ignorant Void — The Ape of Thoth
THE ALL-POWERFUL SLEEPING TITAN — THE DROWNED GREAT FIRE DRAGON
XXIV — THE TITAN AWAKE,
XXV — The Master — of the Dance — MAHAKALA
XXVI — INEFFABLE HEROPAS

functioning Third Eye, is depicted the Tree of Life, with its 16 silver Paths of Darkness, traversed by the Free Will of Man's Spirit, retracing the Route of the Lightning Flash back to its source. Above it are the symbols of the seven planets (right to left): Saturn, Mars, Jupiter, Sun, Venus, Moon, and Mercury, indicating a special sequence of the days of the week: Saturday, Tuesday, Thursday, Sunday, Friday, Monday, and Wednesday. We do not know what the other four faces of the cube show, if anything.

With his left hand, even though in a deep coma, the Titan is strangling, or at least holding at bay, a multicolored Dragon who is vainly attempting to bite off the Titan's head. The winged worm's tail is tightly coiled around the thighs and herculean sex organs of the colossus, from between whose legs arises a rainbow which stretches up through the water and then through the air, until it just touches an eight-pointed Star at the zenith. Below the Star floats an Ark, which could be Noah's, judging from its size and shape, marked with the letter Mem. From the other side of the Star, a smaller rainbow descends and just touches the surface of the water, midway between the Ark and the Sun, rising from Capricorn. At the same time, at the opposite edge of the surface of the sea, a waning Moon is setting in Aries.

Through the many publications by the late Israel Regardie and others of almost all the rituals of the Hermetic Order of the Golden Dawn, it is now openly known that at the ceremony of advancement to the high grade of Adeptus Major, the presiding chief of the Second or Inner Order of the Golden Dawn revealed to the new adept the existence of this mysterious Arcane Key, hitherto hidden from profane mankind.

This is what the new initiate into occult knowledge was solemnly told:

> You have bravely travelled through seven of the twelve steep steps up the Mountain of Knowledge, out of the Valley of Darkness and Ignorance as a raw *Neophyte*, through the increasingly instructing roles of *Pereclinus de Faustis, Poraios de Rejectis, Monocris de Astris, Pharos Illuminans* and *Dominus Liminis*, until you reached, through your own unrelenting efforts, the Kingdom of the *Filius Natus vel Filius Datus* and are now a fully fledged *Adeptus Minor*, standing on the threshold of the state of one who is *Parepidemus Vallis et Doulos Silentii*, with access to further illumination as a Candidate to the High Grade of *ADEPTUS MAJOR*. Therefore I am permitted to wake you and to bring back much that you should remember with the help of the Goad that is LAMED, which brings you to the next step towards the summit, nearer to your Divine Father, Whose very Life is your own.

Remember that the letter MEM, the 13th in the alphabetical sequence, occupies the middle position in the series of the Three Mothers. It is said in the school of the Zohar that its open operation is through the descent of its influence to the abyss, and thus it restrains the rising of those great waters by which the Earth would otherwise again be inundated. In its closed operation, it restricts the power of judgment from the downward course thereof. It is also said that it is like a vessel which in turn is sealed and unsealed, according as there is inhibition or indulgence of its influx to the emanations which are below. In our own Rosicrucian system, the symbolism of MEM is developed after a peculiar manner in its correspondence with the 12th Key of the Tarot. With the more general import of the Hanged Man you will be already familiar, but now you are invited to regard it after a new manner, unavailable to the profane, which can still be brought into harmony with the previous forms of interpretation, since it is simply an advance thereon. Such a Self-sacrifice and free offering, voluntary and joyful, which are ascribed to it in our Tarot teaching, are here connected with the Divine death, with the sacrifice of God Himself, for God must die in order that Man shall live, and thus will not only seek, but find God and bring Him back to Life, to goad us ever higher up the ladder of Man's Destiny.

Remember that the symbolism with which we are here dealing also recalls the Apocalyptic figure of the Lamb slain from the foundation of the world,[10] and thus tells us, in correspondence with previous explanations, that the primary misfortune of the Universe, which is exoterically called the "Fall of Man," exercises a species of incomprehensible compulsion upon the Divine Nature, so that the scheme, of old familiar to everyone under the name of Redemption, comes before us in a certain manner as an eternal necessity and as a consequence of the free will of man rather than of God. And it is this Divine suffering through this misfortune that Man should, will, and must learn to alleviate.

Remember the importance which must be attached to understanding thoroughly the deepest Egyptian symbolism which leads us to know that MEM, through the sacrifice of Christ, has analogy with the legend of the dead Osiris, one of whose appellations was "the shipwrecked or drowned Mariner,"[11] even as this terrible Key, which you see now in its true form, represents a drowned Titan.

This most occult Arcanum, now revealed to you, the 23rd Key of our Tarot, is called *The Drowned Sleeping Titan* and is referred to the elemental sign of Water, as the representative on Earth of the all-pervading ONE SPIRIT or SELF, shared by God and man.

In this image, the drowned Titan sleeps, reposing on the rocky bed of the ocean, with the rainbow at his feet, corresponding to that which has been sunk below the phenomenal world by a sacrifice eternally preordained, which, in one of its aspects at least, is the necessary limitation suffered by the Divine Nature in the act of becoming manifest. The Divine, in a word, is drowned in the waters of natural life; and that which in this respect obtains in the external world, obtains also for humanity, wherein the Divine Spark, beyond all plummets of the senses, beyond all reach of the logical understanding, is immersed in the waters of material existence.

The symbol with which we are dealing corresponds to the legend of our Founder, sleeping in the center of the hidden Vault encircled by the Rainbow, as in the Holy of Holies of Israel there was the abiding presence of the Shekinah. We must remember, moreover, that the ocean of phenomenal life supports on its surface the mystical Ark of Noah, which, in one of its aspects, is the Vessel of Correspondences, wherein the types of all things were collected from the wreckage of the old initiations for transmission through a new era to what is to come. In another sense, which is intimately connected with the first, the Ark is the body of man, the ship of humanity, poised on the waters of the world which conceal the Divine within them. It is man, collective and individual, man in possession of his senses and also enclosed by his senses. There is that within him which, during this his time of probation, is put to sleep as deeply as the symbolical Giant. His originally great nature is restricted in the body, after the manner of God in creation. There is yet another aspect in which we may regard the Ark, for by many issues the great symbols open upon the Infinite which they show forth, though it is after the manner of a reversed glass, darkly. It is that sleep which for a time suspends the soul's communication with the externals, that she may receive the influx of the Divine. It is the house of deep contemplation, of fixed, well-directed thought, by which our exit is found for a time, even from thought itself, to the world of true experience.

Remember that in the roof of the Ark of old there was a window through which the Dove passed and repassed, now in frustrated flight, because many wings are beaters at the Golden Gates, now bearing the olive branch of peace, which for us signifies the suspension of the life of the senses. But, in fine, there came an hour when the Dove returned no more, because the aspiration and reaching up of the Soul at length attains its term.

Remember too the Apocalyptic promise to him who overcometh,[12] and that the last conquest is of the logical understanding, so that thought may be reduced by thought to the point at which it vanishes for a period, but returns subsequently, made splendid by the transmutation of a great experience. You know that the natural mind of man is earthly above all things, and that the Path of our ascent of the Mystic Mountain must carry us far from earth, far from the ways and forms of the material mind. You know further, that ordinary thought is wandering and volatile, and this is the Mercury which the Adept is called upon to fix. I have spoken on the Authority of the Alchemists concerning our imprisoned and liberated Mercury, which are also the forms of thought: one of them errant in the Material and confined therein, the other emancipated; the one volatile, the other fixed by wisdom. Their correspondences in Egyptian symbolism are ANUBIS, the Guardian on the Threshold of the Egyptian Tomb and preventing entrance therein, the Mystic Tomb being the Gate of Life; and THOTH, who enables man finally to penetrate HATOR, that is Beauty and Truth. This is the Word, always sought in all initiations, disguised, reversed, hid, transliterated or substituted after all manners, to be recovered finally in the vestures of another sense, as it is said by St. Paul: "We shall not sleep, but we shall all be changed, in a moment, in the twinkling of an eye . . . and the dead shall be raised incorruptible, and we shall be changed."[13] It is in the silence of thought that we shall hear the Word of Life. The Absolute exceeds thought, but, when we are ready, enters to fill the heart, and it is in this way that God is truly with us, now and forever.

Remember also that *dead* Gods are useless, whether named Christ, Mithra or Osiris. If the Titan immersed beneath the great waters can never more waken, there is no need that we should have part in Him, for we are seeking the fuller Life, that Truth and Beauty which are ever ancient yet ever new. But even as in the old legend, the kiss as the true Grand Hailing Sign awakened the Princess from a sleep of 100 years, so is the slumber of the Gods precious to the Soul of the Postulant at the Gate of the Holy of Holies, because of that Center wherein is the utter stillness of a great activity. They are not dead, but sleeping;[14] it is for us to manifest Them without by the penetration of the Center, and it is in this way that the Divine Colossus will awaken within us. It is for this reason that the limbs of the Titan correspond in their posture to a form of the Fylfot Cross, the Solar Swastika, for though he not only appears to be dead, but has suffered a real death, yet he is the Source of Life and Activity in the Universe. For this reason also, the direction of the face of the Titan symbolizes the appeal of God to man, and man's response to His need.[15]

The right place for this Key XXIII seems to be between Arcanum XI —Strength—and XII—the Hanged Man[16]—although logically and for the sake of symmetry (if these apply), it could be the 12th of 23 letters, thus *preceding* Lamed, which, it is clear, is the Key that goads it, that is, wakes the sleeping Giant and brings him back to active life and the awareness of his Divine Being/Function/Obligation. But if there are 27 letters in the Hebrew alphabet, then it could be the 14th one in such a sequence, that is, Mem!

Let us note, though, that the late Israel Regardie and Robert Wang did not illustrate this Major Trump in their joint Tarot deck, although it is said to be a true copy of the cards as originally used by the Golden Dawn in its heyday. Nor does "The Hermetic Tarot," reconstructed and designed by Godfrey Dowson, have this card, in spite of being "based upon the Esoteric Working of the Secret Order of the Golden Dawn."

In the West, the very first Tarot deck known (of which 17 cards still survive) was prepared in 1392 by the master engraver Jacquemin Gringonneur, for use by King Charles VI of France, nicknamed the "Well-Beloved." Historical slander says that King Charles was mad, but recent research does not support this. He turns out to have been a seer and an adept alchemist who left a very valuable treatise called *Oevre Royalle* (in Old French, not Latin), recently reprinted as an appendix to Dominique Ravel's book *L'oeuvre royale de Charles VI* (Le Léopard d'Or, Paris, 1984). The unnumbered card titled "Le Fol" in Gringonneur's deck shows a very large, benevolent-looking Giant with a foolish grin and vacant eyes, playing or juggling with 14 balls on a string. Perhaps the King and his artist knew more about the esoteric Tarot than they have, so far, been given credit for.

More than one contemporary Tarot adept seems to have come to the same conclusion I have, that there must be more than just 22 Major Arcana. So they have added to their decks at least one more card. For instance, the "Initiate's Tarot" (also known as "The Sexual Tarot"), executed and conceived by Frater R. B-B and issued by The Sorcerer's Apprentice in 1982, calls its extra, unnumbered card "The Dragon," attributing it to the astrological "Head and Tail of the Dragon," or the Moon's nodes.

In his strange[17] book *The Game of Life* (Vol. V of the *Future History Series*, Peace Press, Inc., 1979), Timothy Leary postulates that there must be 24 Major Arcana, representing the 24 stages of man's progress from a unicellular organism to the most advanced entity capable of independent traveling among the galaxies without the need of artificial life supports. He has therefore introduced two extra cards, one of which he places before the traditional last card ("The Universe," as he calls it) and the other after it, concluding the series. His 22nd card he calls "Titan Coeus," or "The Black Hole Explorer," and the 24th one "Titan Themis," or "Singularity." Curious that he should have chosen the description "Titan" as part of the titles of both these extra Arcana. Anyway, he is right in thinking that the Tarot as a whole is a coded message to mankind, as I had previously described in my article "Tarot Major Arcana" in *Cosmos*, Vol. II.[18]

There exists in private use at least one Tarot deck of 80 cards! This was revealed by its designer, Francis Clarke-Rowland of Sheffield, England, in his letter to the "Pandora's Box" section of the periodical *The Lamp of Thoth*.[19] He calls these extra cards "The Bridge" and "The Valley" and describes them and their attributions as follows:

> Of my cards, "The Bridge" is the path between Binah and Chesed, visualised as a "bolt from the blue" or a rainbow. It stands for the direct action of the gods in daily life. Upright, it means an infusion of energy and the ability to go on to better things. Reversed, it gives the effect of something beyond your control playing with your life. I use the correspondences of 31 bis for this.
>
> "The Valley" is between Hokmah and Geburah, and visualized as the "valley of the shadow of death," with a light at the far end. In readings, the querent needs to be brave to reach a good result. Reversed, life is getting to be too much and a break is needed. This is 32 bis.[20]
>
> Hebrew lettering does not do so well with 24 paths, but since I use the 24-rune *futhorc* more than Hebrew, this does not bother me.
>
> When the "veil of the abyss" is drawn across the intersection of the "Valley," "Bridge," and "High Priestess," then the eightfold wheel of the year is formed. If you consider each radial to be the power of the opposing Sephiroth coming into the sphere the radial goes to, then a good descriptions of each of our festivals can be derived.[21]

Someone is bound to ask this question: If there are more than the 22 traditional Major Keys, then what are we to make of their correspondences to the Hebrew letters and the paths on the Tree of Life, and of all the associated numerological curiosities?

The answers seem to me to be along the following lines: 1) The numerological curiosities are just that—curiosities. It is possible that it is because of them that 22 was chosen as the number of Major Arcana to be openly revealed. 2) I do not believe that there is a one-to-one correspondence between the Tarot Major Keys and the Hebrew alphabet, which, in any case, must be taken as consisting of 27 and *not* only 22 letters (despite what Hebrew "scholars" might have to say about this). 3) One could also say that *exo*terically there are only 22 trumps, applicable enough to our world and life as they are now, but *eso*terically there could be more Keys, five more at least.

It is evident that more Tarot Arcana must exist, perhaps to a total of 28 Keys in all. Even if there are but three more Arcana to come, this would fit in quite well with Leary's scheme, by the addition of a ninth "Neurogenetic" level (which would be quite consistent with the Nine Angelic Hierarchies or Choirs, as described by Dionysios the Aeropagite, for example). These three additional "neural circuits" have not yet been made known to man so far, perhaps because human language lacks words or concepts to describe and name them, let alone use them.

But let us here and now be bold, if not foolhardy, and anticipate their appearance in due time by giving them the following provisional names/labels/designations: XXIV—Mahakala: The Master of the Dance; XXV—Buddha: The Awakened Titan; XXVI—The Ineffable Heropas.[22]

This completes the set of 27 Arcana in my Cosmos Tarot. The complete list of additional Keys is as follows:

0	—	FURCA THE FOOL
XXII	—	THE APE OF THOTH
XXIII	—	THE DROWNED SLEEPING TITAN
XXIV	—	MAHAKALA: THE MASTER OF THE DANCE
XXV	—	BUDDHA: THE AWAKENED TITAN
XXVI	—	THE INEFFABLE HEROPAS

The four entirely new keys do not simply follow the 23 Arcana sequentially from 0—Furca the Fool—to XXII—The Ape of Thoth. It seems right that the whole series should begin with Mahakala: The Master of the Dance and end with The Ineffable Heropas. There is some difficulty in deciding where to place the other two. After hesitating and trying different positions, it appears best for XXIII—The Drowned Sleeping Titan—to be between XII—The Hanged Man—and XIII—Death. As to XXV—Buddha:

The Awakened Titan—the best location seems to be between IX—The Hermit—and X—The Turning Wheel. But it is quite possible that further study, meditation, and contemplation of the Arcana will indicate better places for them.

And so we must end, at least for now, our speculative flight and return to our Key XXIII—The Drowned Sleeping Titan. This is certainly not an Arcanum for a facile and glib exposition of each of its several symbols. Being the Key to Samadhi and the finding of the Way of Return, it must be repeatedly meditated on and contemplated individually by every aspirant to real knowledge, which cannot be obtained through an intermediary interpreter, however learned and keen to help.

This key's alternative name, "The All-Powerful Great Fire Dragon," refers to the one all-pervading Energy of Life, manifesting itself at the lowest level of the life force as sex energy and at the highest level as the creative energy of will power. A part of it, known as "Kundalini," is often mistaken for the whole. It, too, cannot be adequately dealt with in any language through the limited parameters of mere words; but it can gradually permeate the human mind, through intentional work on self, creating understanding and thus transforming the mental energy of the mind into intellect. This can best be done through the unlimited medium of what, freely undertaken, "Contemplative Meditation" is at the summit of its scale.

Remember: As popular wisdom knows—if at first you don't succeed, try, try, again!

And *here and now* do not forget to *remember yourself*.

So this revealing[23] ends here with grateful thanks to the Great Archangel HRU for everything he has permitted us to learn.

NOTES

1. See David ibn Zimra's *Magen David* (Amsterdam, 1713) and the anonymous *Sepher Temunah* (Lwow, 1892). This information is taken from Gershom Scholem's *On the Kabbalah and Its Symbolism*.

2. See the *Babylonian Talmud* (Treatise *Sabbat*, f°116a) and the *Derashoth* of Ibn Shu'eib (f°63a) (Cracow, 1573). These references are also taken from the above book by Scholem.

3. Even without any mystical aura about it, the disappearance of letters from an alphabet is not a unique, or even uncommon, event. For example, the Greek *digamma*, or *epistemon*, dropped out of that alphabet as a letter long ago, although it continued to be used as the numeral 6 in Old Greek, as can be seen in St. John's Book of Revelation (The

Apocalypse) 13:18, in which it is a part of the "Number of the Beast." In our own "modern" times the Communist Party leaders deleted by decree three letters from the Russian alphabet, leaving only 33 letters remaining. The ancient original Cyrillic alphabet had no less than 44 letter-signs.

4. See also Rev. F. G. Montagu Powell, *Studies in the Lesser Mysteries* (London: Theosophical Publishing House, 1920).

5. Actually, a case can be made for up to 38 letters in the Hebrew alphabet, as will be explained further.

6. Whatever Hebrew speakers and scholars may say, no less than five of their so-called consonants serve as and are vocalized as vowels, either exclusively or when necessary to make a word pronounceable by human vocal cords. The most amazing fact is that the most sacred of the names of God—the "Ineffable Tetragrammaton," YOD-HEY-VAV-HEY—is made up of three of these letters. When Franz von Baader thoroughly examined the "androgeny" of letters and languages, he came to the conclusion that the vowels were the masculine "tincture," while the consonants were wholly feminine! This is well expressed by Professor Antoine Faivre in his *Accès de l'ésotérisme occidental* (Paris: Gallimard, 1986): "The spoken word supposes the production of sounds both active and passive, in which it expands and which contain and define it . . . At the very origin of language there is a superabundance of desire to communicate and at the same time retain its ambiguity: silence is a feminine tincture which, inasmuch as it is the omnipotentiality of all sounds, desires to be filled, defined, and, to achieve this end, excites the production of a sonority, the masculine tincture, which represents the hunger seeking the medium in which it can express itself. The one needs the other to avoid either complete muteness or inarticulate sounds . . . It is obvious that God is thus the vowel par excellence, the vowel sound which, in the superabundance of His sonority determined in the bosom of the intimate exchange between the Three Persons, allows its natural eternal matrix to give form and expression to the consonant of creation."

7. For a list of these "50 Gates of Intelligence" (subdivided into six "orders"), see Athanasius Kircher, *Oedipus Aegyptiacus, Vol. II*, and W. Wynn-Wescott's edition of the *Sepher Yetzirah*, in the *Collectanea Hermetica Series* (New York: Occult Research Press). Note also that the Sanskrit alphabet has 50 letters. As to the decision on whether Hebrew or Sanskrit is the "eldest" or "divine," I leave it in the hands of those who are more competent than I to judge these matters.

8. Let us note in passing that although there are 28 Lunar "houses" or "stations," and, according to W. B. Yeats' *The Vision*, there are also 28 corresponding types of men, only 27 of these types are actually represented on earth.

9. This quotation is taken from my article in *The Lamp of Thoth*, Vol. III, No. 3 (Whole No. 15) (1984). This periodical is edited by Chris Bray and published by The Sorcerer's Apprentice, 4–8 Burley Lodge Road, Leeds, LS6 1QP, Yorkshire, England.

10. "And all that dwell upon the Earth shall worship him, whose names are not written in the Book of Life of the Lamb slain from the foundation of the world. If any man have an ear, let him hear" (Revelation 13:8–9).

11. When T. S. Eliot wrote in *The Waste Land*, "Here, said she,/Is your card, the drowned Phoenician Sailor,/(Those are pearls that were his eyes. Look!)," was it merely "poetic insight" inspired by Ariel's song in Shakespeare's *The Tempest*? Or was Eliot secretly a Major Adept of the Hermetic Order of the Golden Dawn?

12. Revelation 2:7, 11, 17, 26; 3:5, 12, 21; 21:7.

13. 1 Corinthians 15:51–52.

14. Matthew 9:24.

15. This long quotation is from Israel Regardie, *The Complete Golden Dawn System of Magic*, and from another source, who wishes to remain anonymous.

16. Note that XI + XII = XXIII.

17. Strange, but no stranger than most of his other books. Reading Leary, I suffer from a curious sort of half-envious anger, with a sense of inadequacy and rejection of apparent nonsense which is hiding something else that is urgently important. I experience a very similar, though less angry, state when reading the writings of great "mystics," and suspect that, like them, Leary did see and understand something that cannot be translated into human words, but must be experienced by oneself to be comprehended. His "neurologics" is but an approximation, the best approach he has at his disposal, using such knowledge as he has of anatomy, physiology, psychology, and the biological sciences generally. He has skillfully arranged all this into what he calls "the eight neural circuits" of man. I admire his cleverness, but I must say that I cannot agree with most of his interpretations of the Major Arcana, though I admit and accept his postulate that they are a message to humanity concerning our present state and ultimate possibilities.

18. Nicolas Tereshchenko, "Tarot Major Arcana," *Cosmos*, Vol. II, No. 12 (July 1974).

19. Francis Clarke-Rowland, Letter to "Pandora's Box," *The Lamp of Thoth*, Vol. III, No. 5 (Whole No. 17) (August 1985).

20. The numbers "31 bis" and "32 bis" refer to the lines so numbered in the many tables of correspondences in the book *777*, attributed to Aleister Crowley and published under his name, but in fact composed in great part by S. L. MacGregor Mathers and lent by him to Crowley, who never gave it back and later issued it under his own name, with some additions, but without any acknowledgment or even reference to Mathers.

21. The four great Wiccan sabbats or festivals are: Candlemas (February 2), May Eve or Walpurgis Night (April 30), Lammas (August 1), and Halloween (October 31). They correspond to the four yearly Druidic feasts: *Imbolc* or *Oimelc* (Candlemas), *Beltane* (May Eve), *Lughnassadh* (Lammas), and *Samhain* (Halloween).

22. The name Heropas, usually qualified as "merciless," is borrowed from G. I. Gurdjieff's *Beelzebub's Tales to His Grandson*.

23. I wish this word could sound like the "reveille" for mankind and lead all men to seek and find The Truth and The Way of Return.

JAMES WANLESS

Synergy—A Tarot Myth to Live By, Moving into the 1990S

I BELIEVE IT IS VITAL AND TIMELY TO DEVELOP something new that restores our health and gives us a new sense of empowerment. 1990 starts the decade before the millennium. And every decade before a new century, let alone a millennium, is an extraordinary period of revolution. 1990 adds up to nineteen, the Sun. Then one plus nine is ten, Fortune. One plus zero is one, the Magician. So 1990 begins the decade of Sun, Fortune, and Magic. I think, therefore, that we are going to have an incredible outpouring of creative innovation. A great deal of new technology will appear on the external material plane, as well as a lot of new inner-self technologies. Taroists, as practitioners of an inner-self technology, have a responsibility to keep up with the times and offer a product that will appeal to this revolutionary period.

It's interesting that we're moving into a period in which the majority of the United States population is going to be over forty. People are going to want to take much greater care of themselves. They will be looking toward their health, physically and spiritually; they'll be looking toward their homes, their families; toward cocooning and basic holistic care of the self.

So the 1990s will be a period of great need for healing. And Tarot is a healing tonic. It is a healing tool. We Taroists have to see ourselves as healers who offer a healing technology, product, practice, art, whatever appeals to that particular time and people. We have to be magicians. 1990 brings the period of the Magician.

Magicians have influence in their culture because they use the myths, metaphors, and methods of that time and place. I think it is critical for us as Taroists to update the Tarot and to present it in a light appropriate to the modern age. In doing this we can be true healers.

Also, in a time of revolution people are open to empowerment. Opportunities abound. There are fortunes to be made, egos to be enhanced, during revolutionary periods. I really believe women are going to seize power. I absolutely see that. And I see men redefining power and exercising it in a non-traditional way.

People will be looking to be empowered, to find a technology that empowers them. The Tarot can offer tools of empowerment. All of a sudden people see that they are really Magicians and that they do have the power of the Priestess, the wisdom of the Hierophant, the energy of the Chariot, the entrepreneurial ability of Fortune, and so forth. That's an incredible new vision of themselves, and an incredible sense of empowerment comes out of that.

The nineties will require the use of imagination. In keeping with the decade of the Magician, we will be using our imagic mind. Mag—magic—imagination, they all come from the root word "mag," which means "power." It is through the power of our imagination that we can offer an appropriate tool for this period.

And the new tool that will appeal to people will be inner-directed. This is in keeping with the inexorable move toward the millennium of the Goddess. Any way you cut it, if you see the year 2000 as the number 2, that's the Priestess. If you see 2000 as beginning the third millennium, that's the number of the Empress. Either way, it's a return to Goddess energy, which is an inner-directed experience. People will want inner-directed kinds of technologies. To me the Goddess ascends and affirms herself through symbolic acts, through rites and rituals. The Tarot obviously is a symbolic art. It is a female art. Tarot will be in keeping with the return of ritual and of symbolism. The Taroist is in an incredible position to offer to people who are seizing power—primarily women, or men who have tuned into their feminine power—a tool that will have great appeal and effect.

For the Tarot to contribute to more people more effectively, we need to communicate it differently. I think we even need to practice it differently. We have to present the Tarot in a way that appeals to women, so women can find their power through an art that is theirs. Often women try to find their power in a man's way, which doesn't seem very effective. We also have to present a Tarot that appeals to men, to their ego, one that they can find useful in their work. I want to bring Tarot out of the metaphysical book store and into the mainstream, because that's where its real action can be.

"Synergy" is a great word. It's a modern word with ancient roots. It's equated with energy, which by itself is neutral. Most people aren't against energy. I think that as our material resources become more limited, and we proclaim the greatest natural resource to be within the self, "synergy" as a word will have much greater meaning and impact. The concept of synergy is often used in the business world.

"Synergy" is a word derived from the ancient Greek. It means "sun," "ergos," and that means working together. I think the concept of working together is powerful. Synergy means everything, everybody, all the different selves within us, working together. In working together the whole— whether the whole self, the whole relationship, or the whole business—is greater than the sum of its parts. That's what synergy is all about. By unifying all the parts, which is to heal, we increase our power exponentially; we are empowered. So synergy has the two concepts that I think are critical for the nineties—healing and power. The new healing power.

To me, life is a verb. Jim or James, that's static; it doesn't work. I am a verb. I am in process. I am fermenting. I am a work in progress and therefore I should really be Jimmy. I'm Jimmy right now, jimmying ideas together. Maybe you can see that or maybe you can't. I see myself right now as jamming, jim-jamming, something like that. Some people might call me Jack, for jacking around. Taroists might call me a Fool for fooling around, but it's in that process of jimmying, jacking, fooling around, that great insights occur. I think it's important to approach Tarot as a verb, so we can be Taroting. It sounds like a dance. Would you like to Tarot with me? Let's Tarot. We're dancing and Tarot is a dance. What I want to emphasize here is that Tarot is a *process*, to get away from Tarot as a formal noun, to get away from the formal, traditional construct of the Tarot. Let's get into the essence of Tarot. To Tarot, rather than the Tarot. The process of synergizing Tarot emphasizes the heart and soul of Tarot—the individual's relationship to the Tarot's archetypes.

The Major Arcana cards, the court cards, are archetypes. They reflect primal patterns of human personality and behavior. These archetypes are rendered in symbolic imagery. Now, how do we apply this archetypal imagery with Tarot? I see four distinct levels. On the first level I'd have a reading from some Tarot reader. That's first-level Tarot. That's primary. The second level of Tarot is to read for myself. But I still read the meanings from the book. "Oh, what does the book say here?" Second grade. In third-level Tarot I read for myself but I throw away the book. I ask, "What do I see, what do I feel, how does it speak to me?" That's high-level Tarot. But I think there's an even higher level, fourth-level Tarot, which is to create your own archetypal symbols, your own deck. I believe that if you are a serious Taroist and really want "to Tarot," that's what you must do. Now this does not mean you have to publish this deck. It is your deck. It is your private way of relating to the ancient archetypal symbols. To me, this is the highest level of Tarot.

This is the Tarot that ultimately may appeal to the public. I think the public is probably jaded now with the psychic-fair kind of Tarot reading. Maybe this is only true in California, not in other places. But I do think Tarot needs to grow up. We need to offer a mature product, a mature practice. I think the entire New Age, in a sense, needs to grow up. Tarot practitioners have a responsibility to teach people how to become their own best oracle, their own Tarot reader and Tarot creator. That's what's going to appeal to women, because it's such a visual, esthetic art; it's like writing in a journal, doodling, drawing out images from yourself. This may also appeal to men, because suddenly they won't have to go to a psychic reader, someone with mysterious powers. Men don't really like that. They want to satisfy their own ego, do it their own way. So Tarot self-reading appeals to both males and females.

The most important thing about doing your own Tarot is that self-generated symbolism leads to what the great psychologist Carl Jung called individuation, which is becoming whole. One way to become whole and individual, to find your true self, is to find your own way of relating to archetypal symbols. Nobody else can do it for you. Many of us will write books, but books are written by authors for themselves, to explain things to themselves. Authors are people who simply have enough ego to think other people might relate to what they say. But the idea is to find it for yourself. You can read a book, throw it away and find your own path. That's the way to become individual. The word "individual" means "whole," "undivided." If I'm buying into somebody else's belief system or symbolism, I'm not me. Who am I? I'm not authentic. People ask me why I made the Voyager deck. It was because I couldn't relate to someone else's medieval symbols. They didn't mean anything to me. I felt that to be authentic and responsible I had to create my own symbology, and then if other people liked it, great. But it was really for me.

Now why place so much emphasis on archetypes? It's because the Major Arcana archetypes compose the very structure of our psyches. Every state we are in, every role we act out, is archetypal. You can name and put a character to every feeling and every action. So right now we're playing out the archetypal role of what? Teacher? Hierophant? The receptive Moon? Or the active Sun? When I wake up in the morning I'm the Fool, I don't know what's going on today, this is zero. What do I do today? I have no idea, a blank mind. Then somebody calls me and I have to communicate on the Magician level immediately. They want to know something, and I have to be the Priestess. I have to call up my memory. Then I have to take care of my body, my physical needs, I have to eat. I'm the Empress nurturing myself. Then I handle some business. I'm the Emperor. Then I do a reading, and all of a sudden I'm the Hierophant. My girlfriend comes into my life and I am the Lovers. When I go downtown, I get into my Chariot and drive there. When I'm tired, I go home and I'm the Hermit. Maybe a check has come in the mail; then I'm Fortune. On and on, you go through every action. Every part of your day is archetypal; that's why it's so important. Discovering the different archetypal selves within you is what the easterners call self-realization. It is discovering all the selves which compose the higher self, the whole self.

Synergistic Tarot is a lot like the ancient path of alchemy. In alchemy you take the natural ingredients—air, fire, water, and earth—and you blend them. You're the chef of your life, and your life is the soup. What are you going to create with this concoction? Well, you create who you are, your individuality, your wholeness. In synergistic Tarot you are interested in how to relate to the archetypal elements of the Tarot—the Magician, the Priestess, and so forth—how to blend them, how to create your life through them. That's what makes you whole—the blending, the weaving. The chef that you are is all-important.

One of the nice things about archetypal psychology like this is that not only does it bring in Jung's process of individuation, traditional psychology, as well as Eastern self-realization, mystical European alchemy, and all, but it's also fun. It's entertaining. It's fantasy—to see yourself as a Magician and watch this movie of all your different selves. Your Amazon warrior self, interacting suddenly with your Cinderella self, with your medicine-woman self, and all the other different selves. They battle and they struggle and they embrace and they love. It's theater. It's the best theater of all. That's why it's easy to be a hermit. Who needs to go to a movie theater when you have all this action? It's all there—comedy, tragedy, adventure, the whole thing—going on within you.

I think the public could like this if it were presented properly. Look at yourself and see all the weird, comic cartoon-type figures that you are. Develop the fantasy. Why do you have to see it on the big screen? Why pay for it when it's all in your mind? This idea of finding your archetypal selves appeals to the ego. Ego is not just a bad thing, it's a great tool, because ego is self. It's me, and now if I can find all these different me's, that's even more exciting. So you can use this to enhance your ego. But it's a trick, seeing all the other different selves you are. At some point you think, Who am I, really? That's an interesting question. I think we are always in the process of changing and putting on different roles. We are a verb. I am not Jim. I'm sorry, I was Jim a minute ago, but now I'm Jam. And then back to Jack and the Fool and so on.

Then there's the matter of being goddesses and gods. Women are goddesses these days finally. They are finally acknowledging the goddesses that they are. Men have not seen the gods that they are. Let's face it, men don't have a clue about the gods within them. The archetypal selves within us are the gods and goddesses. Jean Bowling, who wrote *The Goddess in Every Woman*, is now coming out with *The God in Every Man*. How we're waiting for that one!

How do you access these different archetypal selves? How can you get in touch with them? In synergistic Tarot there are two basic methods: First of all, you visualize them, you see them; second, you talk to them. You use your right-brain imagination. "Oh, look at you, Mr. Magician self.'' Then you talk with your left brain to that self. You put verbal content behind the vision that's there.

When you see a different archetypal self within you, it is absolutely essential to draw it out physically. Put it down on paper—draw it or write it out—make a sound for it, make a dance to it, act it out, cry to it. Do something on the physical level, otherwise it won't work. I think it's especially important for you to try to draw it out. Even if you're not an artist, draw anyway. The results will amaze you. Studies have shown that if you pick an emotion, like anger, and everybody draws it, seventy-five percent of the illustrations are almost the same. So there is something archetypal in the whole process of drawing. If you want to draw out your archetypal selves, you literally draw them out. You don't have to have even a vision of them before you start drawing. Let your hands do the walking and talking here; just let go and see what happens. A good book for this is *Drawing on the Right Side of the Brain*, by Betty Edwards. But she has a sequel which I think is more important philosophically, *Drawing on the Artist Within*. I'm a klutz at drawing. But that doesn't matter. The point is to just draw.

It's fortunate that the picturing process, drawing and visualizing, is becoming increasingly popular. You see it used in sports and business now. Sports figures, business people, are visualizing themselves being successful in an active negotiation, or up at the plate, or wherever. Obviously, picturing is very important in hypnosis. I think the real vogue in self-help tools of the nineties is going to be art therapy, although I don't like the term. But I think it's just going to explode. People are going to start drawing, painting, sculpting. We're going to reacquaint ourselves with the artists within. One of the principles of synergistic Tarot is to use other techniques with which we are comfortable to bring it all together. If art therapy, drawing these things, works, then let's use it. I go around to imagery conferences and art therapy conferences just to see what they're doing.

Then there's the left-brain process of writing it down. If I'm looking for my Magician, and I see him and draw it out, then I want to talk to my inner Magician. I want to see what he has to say. When I talk to him, I want to write it down—that's exceedingly important. When you write it down it's as if you've stamped it in your physical consciousness; then you begin to act on it in the material world. A good book for talking to your inner archetypal selves is a new one by William Johnson called *Inner Work*. Johnson is a Jungian psychologist, and he has a chapter that's half on dreams and half on active imagination, in which as he tells you point by point exactly how to talk to your inner self. It's an excellent guide. In any event, the key to synergistic Tarot is imagination, because it is through your imagination that you can contact your inner self. Einstein said that imagination is more important than knowledge. That's why it doesn't matter if you know what all the books on Tarot say—that's wonderful and I respect that—but I want to see a person's imaginative self use all that knowledge. That to me is the process.

The beauty of the imagination is that it's free. Everybody has it and everybody uses it. Most of the time we just daydream with it. Instead, let's direct it. Let's use our imagination. When you're driving for hours on the freeway or you're stuck in traffic, direct your imagination to one of these inner archetypal characters and have a conversation. You may even want to record it while you're doing it.

I want to describe my own experience with this inner process of accessing archetypal selves. So many people who consult Tarot symbology have relationship problems of one kind or another. My relationship problem was not a lack of wonderful women. There are incredible women in the world. It's unbelievable. My problem was the familiar male dilemma, inability to commit to one of them. I used to tighten up. It's a traditional male problem. Now, an axiom of the Tarot is that if you have a problem on the outside level, look inside because that's where the source of the problem is. This lack, my inability to commit, had been getting me into trouble. I didn't feel good about it. I was in pain, I suffered. People don't believe that, but it's really true. So, I had to come to terms with that. I had not been really happy, although it appeared that everything was fine. I had to begin looking inward, looking at the archetypal guidance of the Tarot. I felt intuitively that my unwillingness to commit came from the struggle between my inner child and my inner male adult. My inner child is the kid in me, the Page, Prince, Princess—in the Voyager deck it's called the Fool Child—the young expression in the Tarot deck, the archetypal child. The inner male adult is the archetype of the Emperor. So the struggle was between the Fool Child and the Emperor. The Emperor is number four, and if you look at the Fool as twenty-two, it also adds up to four. It's an interesting duality, the traditional zero/twenty-second Fool Child and the Emperor, and I sensed that there was a real battle going on between those two. My child self, the Fool, is really a free spirit and wants no part of commitment; it wants zero commitment. My adult self, however, the Emperor archetype, would really like to build a solid relationship based upon a commitment. They are at loggerheads.

So what to do? Going back to the key of synergistic Tarot, I used my imagination. Ah ha, let me figure this one out here. I don't need to read all the books. Let me look at a couple of books and take it from there. Using my imagination, I went inside to meet my Fool Child self and I started a dialogue. I started to talk with my inner child, and I said, "What do you think of commitment?" It was brutal. My child self said, "Well it's adult stuff, boring, suffocating, deadly." Those were the words that came out. I then asked my inner adult Emperor what he felt about my childlike lack of commitment. His response was also pretty brutal. He said that if I did not commit, then I would continue to be superficial like the child. Oh, that bothered me. Never getting past the physical level bothered me, too. I'm working in metaphysics, I'm supposed to be beyond just the physical level. My adult Emperor said I was a Fool for not seeing all the potentials

and possibilities of a committed relationship and the wonders that such depth could bring to me. He said that I would never realize the supreme, fulfilling joy of going deep, deep, deep with another—I had always been going out, out, out.

After that dialogue I saw the conflict clearly. Next, I evoked my imagination to picture my Fool Child's view of adulthood. I wanted to draw it out. My kid self sees my adult self. What's the picture of the adult? I had no idea, but here's the picture I drew: square-looking horse, almost like a robot. My child was telling me that this was his view of being an adult. My child self said that adulthood was for squares. The *square* horse was for conventional robotic types of people who just did what society expected them to do, workhorses who did not really know how to live.

Then I asked my Emperor adult to draw a picture of how he saw my Fool Child self. What appeared was unbelievable, a face with just one large eyeball and a big gaping mouth, with outstretched arms and a body moving, grasping, reaching, stretching for something, moving at a rapid pace to consume experience. My adult self was saying that my child self could never be happy and at peace, that he was always seeking a new thrill, a new experience to consume. At this point, I knew I was in deep, and this was painful, but it was also entertaining. My Emperor self liked it because it was serious. My child self liked it because it was fun—pictures and struggles and archetypal conflicts and things like that. It would be interesting to see what George Lucas would do with something like this.

I was shocked by the severity of the conflict. I saw that the place where we are dysfunctional in the world is a product of a deeper inner conflict between our archetypal opposites. Synergistic Tarot requires that you have a dialogue with your different selves, your opposite selves, in order to be healed. Synergistic Tarot is healing work. You heal the Fool Child and the Emperor, and in healing the two, you become empowered. Healing creates power, but you have to have a dialogue with the opposites for that healing to occur.

I also learned that drawing and having a dialogue, the two processes of the right and left brains, contribute amazingly to each other. When I drew the picture, I got a whole new set of words. This new set of words created almost a new image, modified the old picture.

It is also absolutely vital to see clearly both the positive and negative sides of your different archetypal selves. It became necessary to ask my Fool Child self what he saw positively about himself after my Emperor self had disparaged him. I wanted to know what he thought was good about himself. So I asked my Fool Child to draw a picture of himself. And here is what emerged, a beautiful little smiling face set inside a seed blowing in the wind. My Fool Child was telling me that it is the source of my creativity, the source of my wonder, my freshness, my energy, my aliveness. That thrilled me, and so I respected that.

But then I had to also ask how my inner Emperor viewed himself positively. My Emperor's hand drew a male figure, an "holistic self" figure, inside an apple, with arms and legs extending to the four corners of the apple. My adult self said to me that this picture of the whole man inside the apple was a symbol of his maturity. The mature apple symbolized his fullness, his sufficiency, his success, his power, his ability to nurture all the qualities of the adult Emperor male. That made me feel great and gave me lots of strength and confidence. Now I had the positive picture.

Once the dualities had been exposed for both of these contradictory archetypes, I then had to heal them. Here were the differences; now how could I resolve them? So I asked each of them how they felt we could resolve the conflict, how we could reach an accommodation. My Fool Child self said that he didn't mind me, James, my ego-self James, being an adult so long as my Fool Child self was respected. There should be time allotted for play, for spontaneity and fooling around. He said, "You can be an adult, but respect my time to play and be a fool. And when the time is right to play, I don't want that time taken away. I want respect for it."

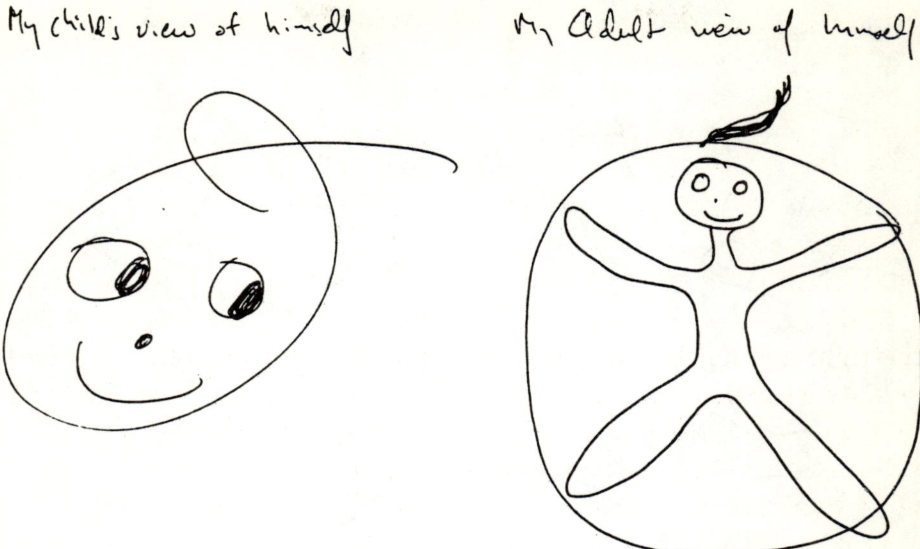

Then I asked my Emperor adult self how he felt we could reach an accommodation with my kid and he said that he wanted trust from the child. The Emperor was willing to honor the child's playtime request, but at the appropriate time. "Let's play, but play when it's the right time to play." And that all made sense to me.

Then I asked each of these two selves how they pictured this healing resolution. This time my picture of the Fool Child was the same little smiling face inside the seed, but the seed was held within a hand, a soft hand, and I saw that it was the hand of the Emperor. The Fool Child self was telling me he wanted the security and stability, the warmth and affection and guidance and compassion of my inner adult. He really wanted that father within me to work for him. And I was very touched by this; it actually made me cry. I think it's necessary to *feel* the process. It's not just intellectual work, it's letting the feelings come out. It could be a cry, a scream, a laugh, whatever it might be, a twitch, I don't know, it doesn't make any difference, but let your feelings flow. It's absolutely an important principle of doing this kind of work.

Now what about my adult's picture of the healing resolution? This time I had the adult in the apple, but placed in the heart of the adult was the little child seed. So the adult was saying, "I am an adult in the world but a child at heart." That made me feel great, that I can come from that place of the child but still be in the world like the Emperor. And again I

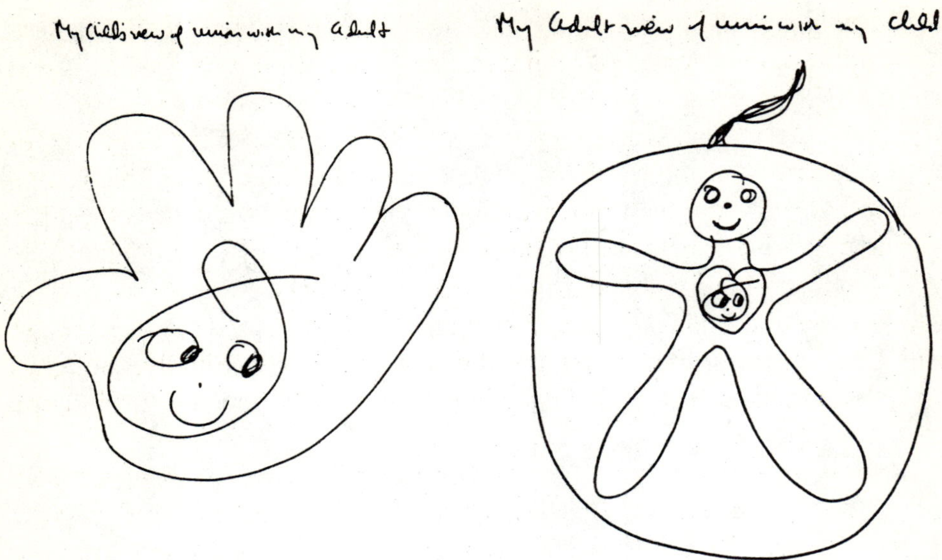

was profoundly moved. From this whole inner conversation an amazing realization came to me. I understood for the first time that I can be an adult and make adult-like commitments without losing my child-like need for play and freedom. I can have both. I realized that both my child and my adult, my Fool and my Emperor, needed each other for their own greater fulfillment. Working like an adult to realize the apple-fruits of my endeavors will allow me to play freely and guiltlessly. As an adult, I get things done; then I can forget about that and go play without guilt. Then in playing, my child side is completely satisfied and releases me to go back to being an adult. This is incredible for me. Finally, a resolution for all of this!

Pieces of my inner-relationship puzzle remained unsolved, however. Not only did I need to heal my child with my adult self, but to grow up and be able to commit, I also had to synergize my inner male with my inner female, to heal my relationships with women. The need for this integration is implicit in the Tarot, with the feminine Moon card and the masculine Sun card next to each other. So I pursued the same synergistic process between my Sun male and Moon female as between my child and adult selves. There was a conflict between my inner male and my inner female. I had to find out who I was as a man, which meant I had to go back to the time when I first saw myself as a male vis-a-vis my primary male role model, my father, the King. And I had to look at the first time I saw myself as a male vis-a-vis a female, which was my mother, the Queen. In recalling the mother and father of my childhood, I realized I had an often-absent father and a very controlling mother. As a result, my maleness was stunted. (If you want to read a great book about men as kids, read *Puer Eternis* by Marie von Franz.) Therefore, I had to access my inner father and my inner mother. Everybody has these within them. I was able to find a very nurturing, involved father and an unconditionally loving mother inside me. Out of this process I realized that at age forty-five, unbelievably, I was really still at the stage of the teenager. In between child and adult, between son and man. You can just imagine my pictures of the teenager —the Chariot, the self in transition, the in-between self. Finally, though, I was able to see and feel myself growing up from child and son to adult and man.

It was amazing to me to see that in this process of drawing it out, I had in effect created my own inner family. I had created a new Fool card, not the Voyager Fool card. I had created an Emperor card, my Emperor adult-self card. I had created a male card, in the sense of the Sun. I had created a new feminine card, in the sense of the Moon. I had created a card being the son in the family, which might be the Prince or something like that. I had in effect created seven different Tarot cards out of this individual inner exploration and healing process. And that's the way to create a deck. Or you can just simply start talking to your Magician and see what your Magician looks like. Draw it out and you have your card. As you draw these cards, you can laminate them, so they'll last. Put them in a form where you can use them; then every day, select a card. A card a day keeps the shrink away. A card a day is the simplest, easiest kind of entertainment—and that's what we need, to be entertained. When you do this, you remember yourself. You need to remind yourself who you are, because much of the time you are not culturally supported in this. A card a day can remind you of who you are.

As I continue to mature, my images change and I redraw the cards. I believe your Tarot decks should reflect your maturation. Keep your Tarot, your symbology, current with your own growth, and in doing this you stay in the moment and you stay in the process. You are not caught up in Tarot as a noun, but see it as a verb, and see yourself as a verb. And when you are in the moment, as a process, as a verb, then you cannot help but grow. And that's what life is all about. Just growing.

CONTRIBUTORS

HILARY ANDERSON, Ph.D., is a lecturer and seminar leader in East-West psychology and religion, and has specialized in transformational work with Tarot and other oracular traditions for over twenty years. She is on the faculty of National University, teaching psychology, and she maintains a private consulting practice in Los Angeles. Dr. Anderson contributes articles to magazines, and her new book is on *Integral Yoga Psychology* (to be published in 1989). She currently is finishing a book on Tarot imagery, *The High Priestess Speaks on Tarot*, which presents a new, multidimensional perspective. This book is to be published in 1990.

ANGELES ARRIEN, a native Basque raised biculturally, is an author, anthropologist, educator, and corporate consultant. Her teachings are based on the universality of values, ethics, and experiences as they relate to myths, symbols, and the arts. She lectures internationally and has taught over 400 workshops in cross-cultural anthropology and transpersonal psychology at colleges, universities, and humanistic growth centers. Angela also offers a year-long cross-cultural shamanic training course ("The Four-Fold Way") and has a private practice in personal growth consultation. Her publications include *The Tarot Handbook: Practical Applications of Ancient Visual Symbols* (Arcus Publishers, 1987). She lives in the San Francisco Bay area.

EILEEN CONNOLLY, Ph.D., is an internationally acclaimed parapsychologist and authority on Tarot and Gnothology, the esoteric science of numbers. Born in England, she and her husband Leo and their six children moved to the United States in 1968. Her books (all published by Newcastle) include: *Tarot: A New Handbook for the Apprentice (The Connolly Tarot, Vol. I); Tarot: The Handbook for the Journeyman (The Connolly Tarot, Vol. II); The Connolly Book of Numbers,*

Vol. I: The Fundamentals; The Connolly Book of Numbers, Vol. II: The Consultant's Manual; and *Earthdance*, a novel about reincarnation. Forthcoming books include: *Karma Without Stress; Karma, Destiny and the Numbers of Children*; and *Tarot: The Handbook for the Master (The Connolly Tarot, Vol. III)*. Dr. Connolly is also the creator of "The Connolly Tarot Deck," scheduled for release in 1989. She now resides in Virginia, where she is President of the Connolly University of Parapsychology and an adjunct professor at Atlantic University. She is a regular guest on television and radio and conducts seminars and workshops in cities worldwide.

GAIL FAIRFIELD has been a full-time professional Taroist and astrologer since 1980. Her work has included private consultation, teaching small and large classes, tutorials, and conference seminars. She has written *Choice Centered Tarot* (Newcastle, 1985) and has several new books in progress. Gail's current focus is on writing and tutoring those who want to become professional in Tarot or astrology. She lives in Seattle with a variety of human and animal friends.

MARY KATHERINE GREER is a writer and teacher of methods of self-exploration and transformation. She is the author of three books on the Tarot, each an experiential workbook: *Tarot for Your Self: A Workbook for Personal Transformation* (Newcastle, 1984); *Tarot Constellations: Patterns of Personal Destiny* (Newcastle, 1987); and *Tarot Mirrors: Reflections of Personal Meaning* (Newcastle, 1988). Tools and Rites of Transformation (T.A.R.O.T.) is a learning center directed by Miss Greer for the study of divination, women's mysteries, and the transformative arts. She leads shamanic and magical workshops in women's moon-time traditions. In addition to her twenty years of reading, studying, and teaching the Tarot, she has been an editorial assistant, typesetter, graphics designer, college administrator, and Professor of English and Women's Studies. A world traveler who has lived in Japan, Germany, England, and Mexico, as well as in six states in the U.S., Mary now lives in Nevada City, California, when she is not on the road or lecturing.

AMBER JAYANTI, author of *Living the Tarot* (Newcastle, 1988), is an internationally known practical mystic who has been living, studying, consulting with, and teaching the Tarot for over twenty years. She is a member of Builders of the Adytum, a school for Tarot and Qabalah study founded by the late Paul Foster Case. In 1975 Swami Muktananda Paramahansa gave Amber her last name, Jayanti, meaning "victory," after he initiated her into Siddha Yoga. Her new work in progress is *Tarot and Qabalah for the 21st Century*.

WILLIAM LAMMEY'S career, which has included being a Navy Civil Engineer Officer and twenty years as a licensed architect, has led him to live in such distant places as Hawaii and Belgium. Now 48, he lives in Austin, Texas, where he writes and teaches and reads the Tarot. His current courses include two at the Austin Community College, "The Tarot" and "Beginning Metaphysics," and national seminars. He is the author of *Karmic Tarot: A New System for Finding and Following Your Life's Path* (Newcastle, 1988). Mr. Lammey currently is completing two new books, one on the metaphysical causes of illness and the other entitled *The Architecture of Spirituality: Building a Philosophy of Life*.

RACHEL POLLACK was born in Brooklyn and raised in Poughkeepsie, New York. She is the author of eleven books, including *78 Degrees of Wisdom* (2 vols.); *Salvador Dali's Tarot; The Haindl Tarot*, and other works on the Tarot and divination. She also has written three novels, the latest being *Unquenchable Fire*. Her new books are *The New Tarot*, a study of contemporary Tarot decks, and *Tarot Tales*, an anthology of stories edited with Caitlin Matthews. Rachel Pollack's work has been translated into French, German, Spanish, Dutch, and Danish. She has lived in Amsterdam, Holland, for the past fifteen years.

NICOLAS TERESHCHENKO was born in 1916 in Russia, studied in Serbia and Paris, qualified in medicine at King's College, London, and was then commissioned in the Indian Medical Service. Throughout this odyssey, from childhood on, he was intrigued with all occult matters, wondering about the purpose of life, and gathering information from all the books and teachers he could find. Eventually he saw that his main interest lay in several fields of esotericism. He now divides his time between Gurdjieff's work (about which he wrote *A Look at Fourth Way Work*) and the teachings of the Builders of the Adytum. His other books include *Fragments de Gnose* and *Les Trésors du*

Tarot, and his articles have appearaed in French, English, and Australian periodicals. He now lives in Paris and teaches and counsels in the United States, and is the creator of "The Cosmos Tarot Deck." He currently is writing *The Minor Arcana of the Tarot*, a book intended to accompany his first Tarot volume. He also is doing a study of the Hermetic Order of the Golden Dawn and its manifestation in France and writing another book on the Fourth Way, based on Gurdjieff's *Beelzebub's Tales to His Grandson* and the reconciliation of the terminologies used by Gurdjieff and Ouspensky.

JAMES WANLESS, Ph.D., a professional symbolist, is the creator of "The Voyager Tarot Deck" and author of *New Age Tarot* and *The Way of the Great Oracle*. Dr. Wanless lectures and counsels nationally and directs the Voyager School of Symbolism, with a correspondence course in symbolism and Tarot, and multimedia workshops. He is the founder of Merril-West Publishing, which produces books on symbolism, art, games, cassettes, conferences, and a catalog of New Age tools and toys called *The Magic and Mystery Guide*. He is also the co-founder of the Association of Symbolic Arts. Dr. Wanless lives and maintains a consulting practice on the Monterey Peninsula in California.